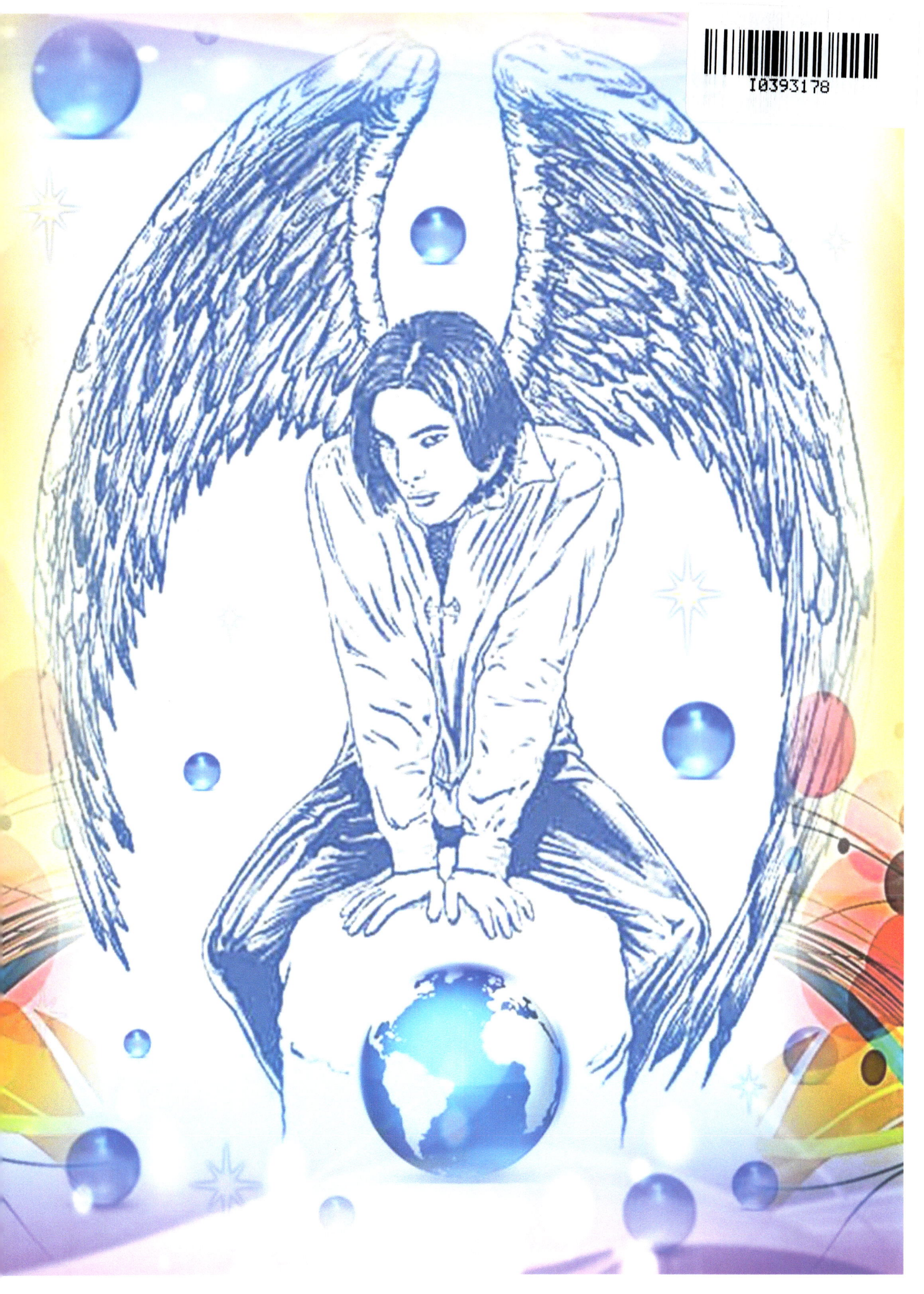

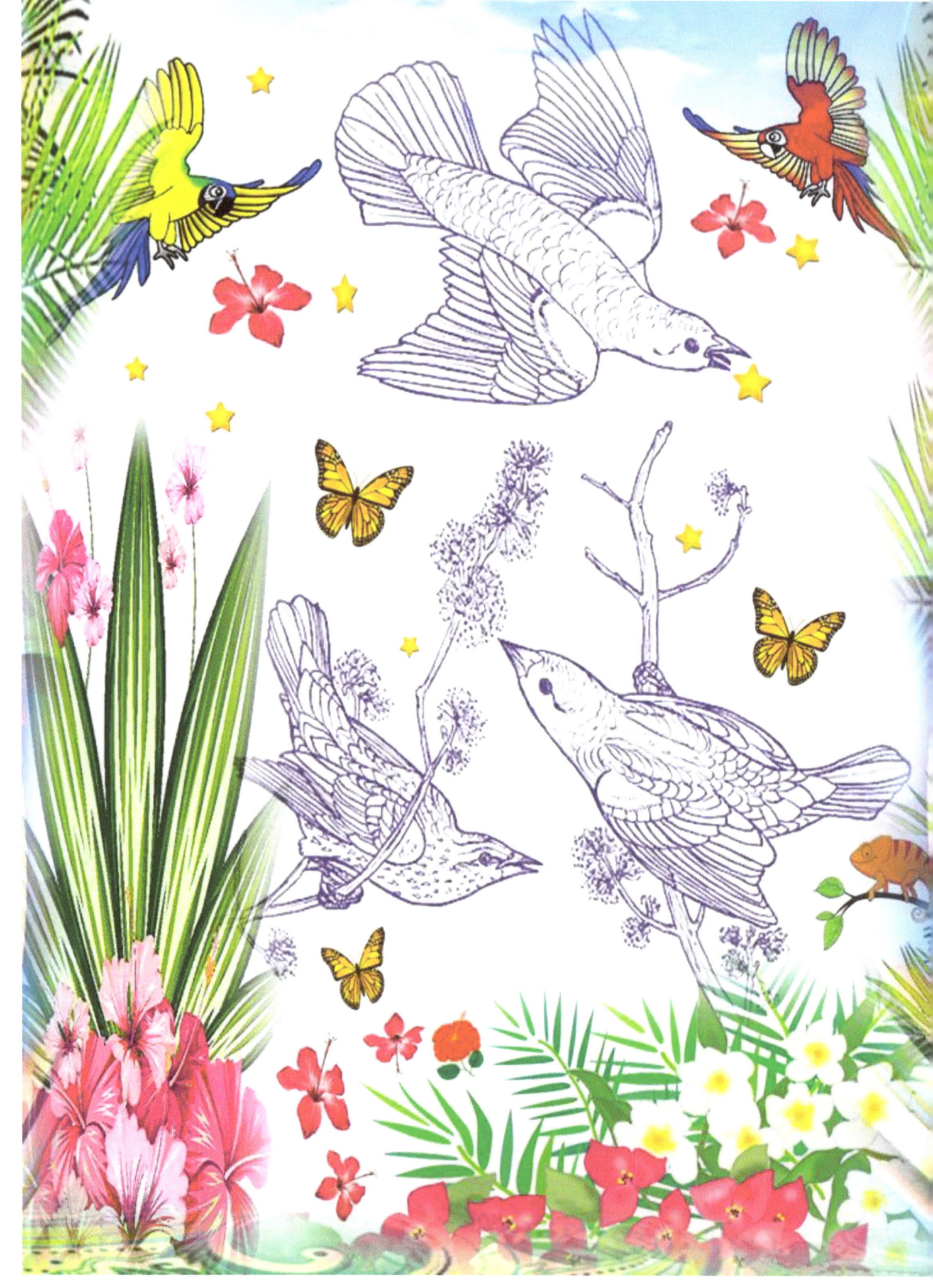

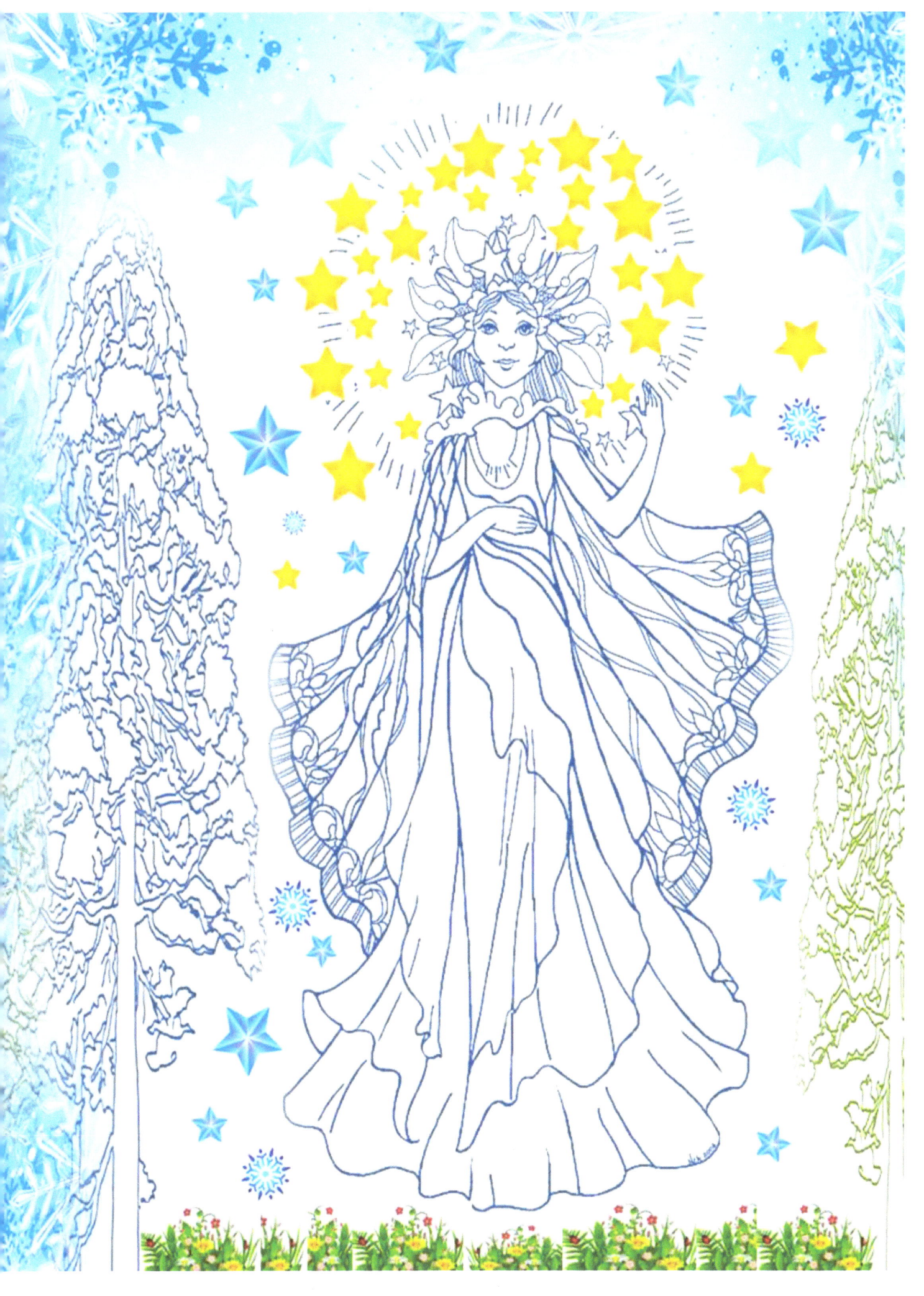

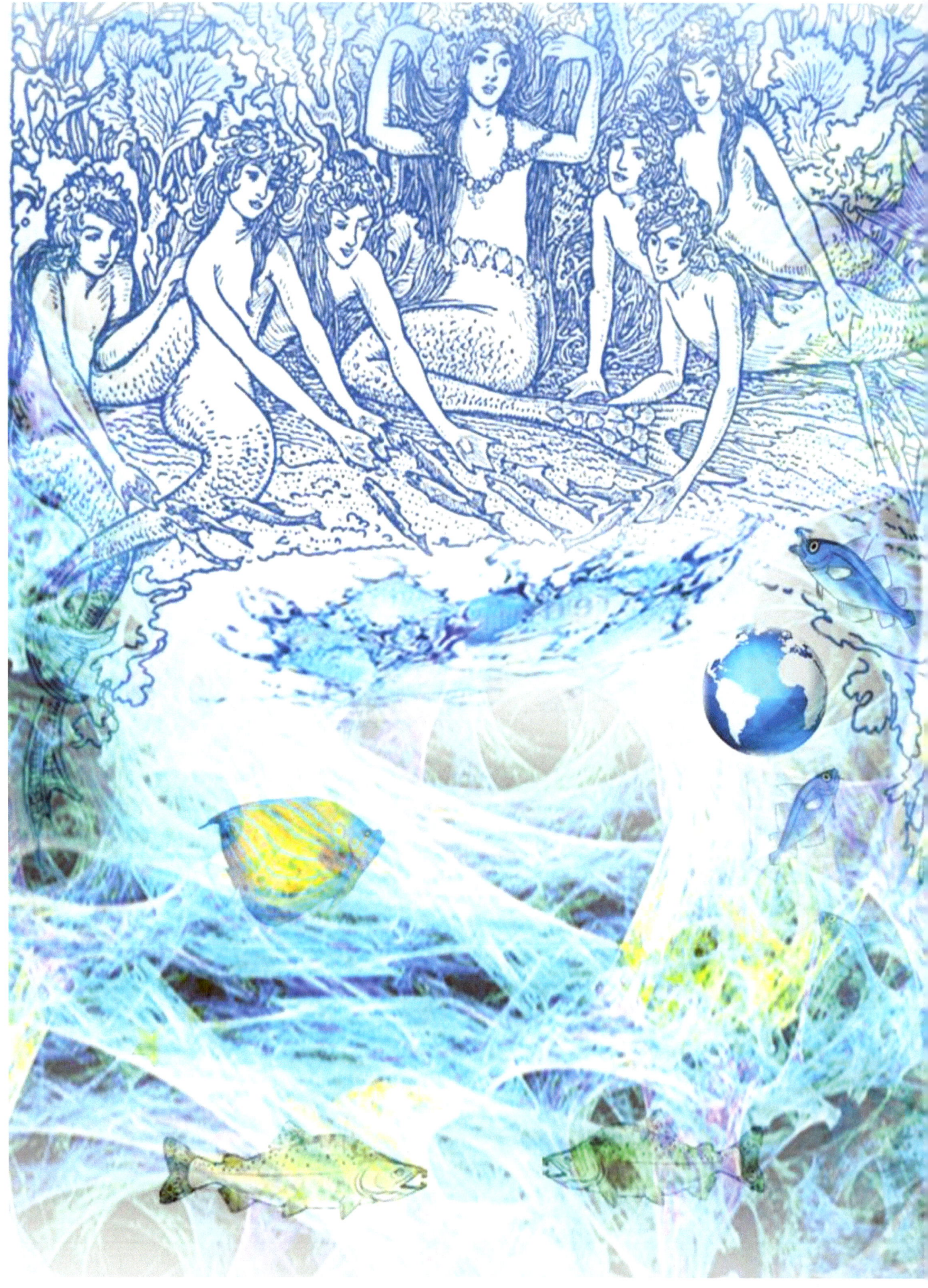

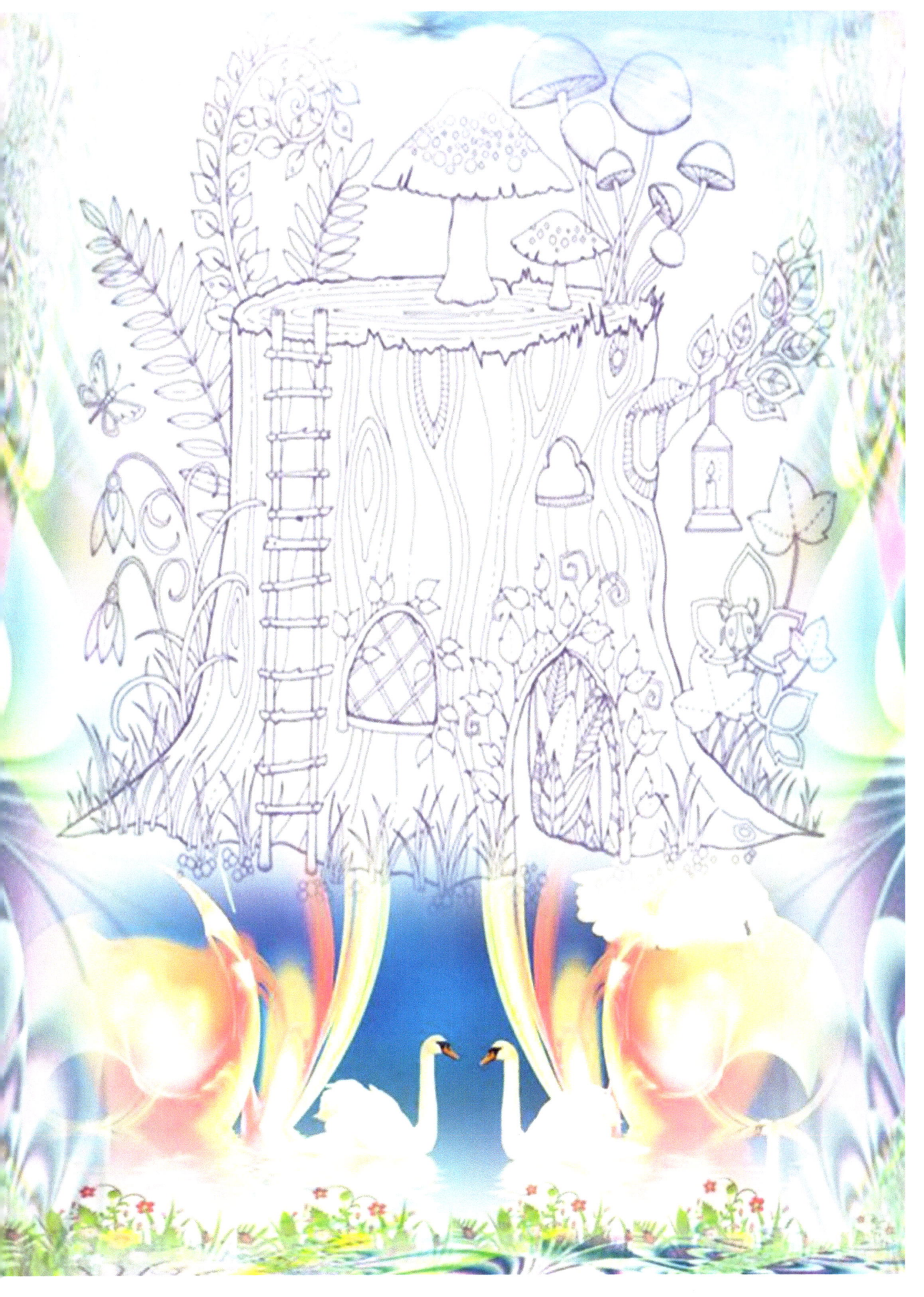

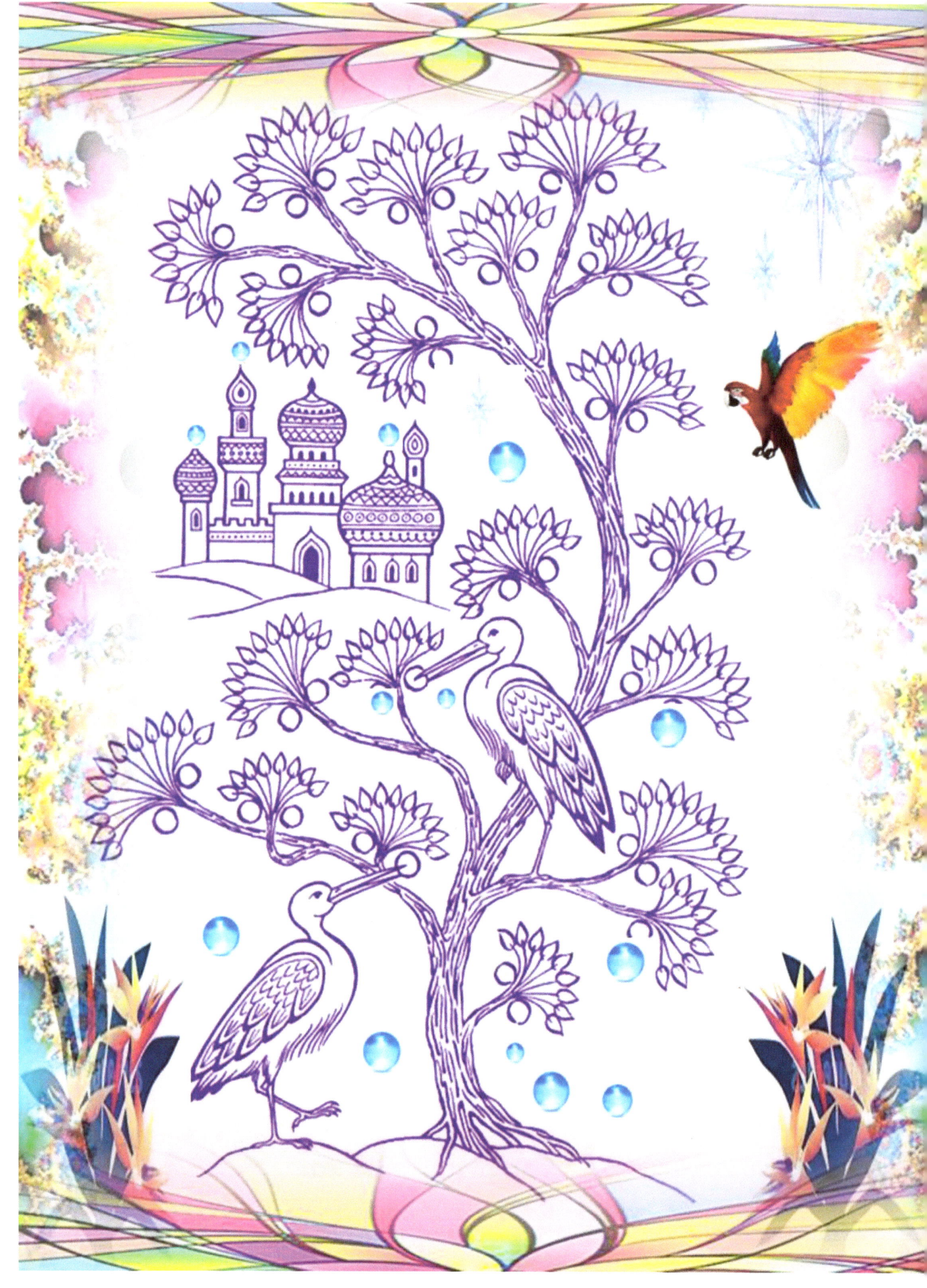

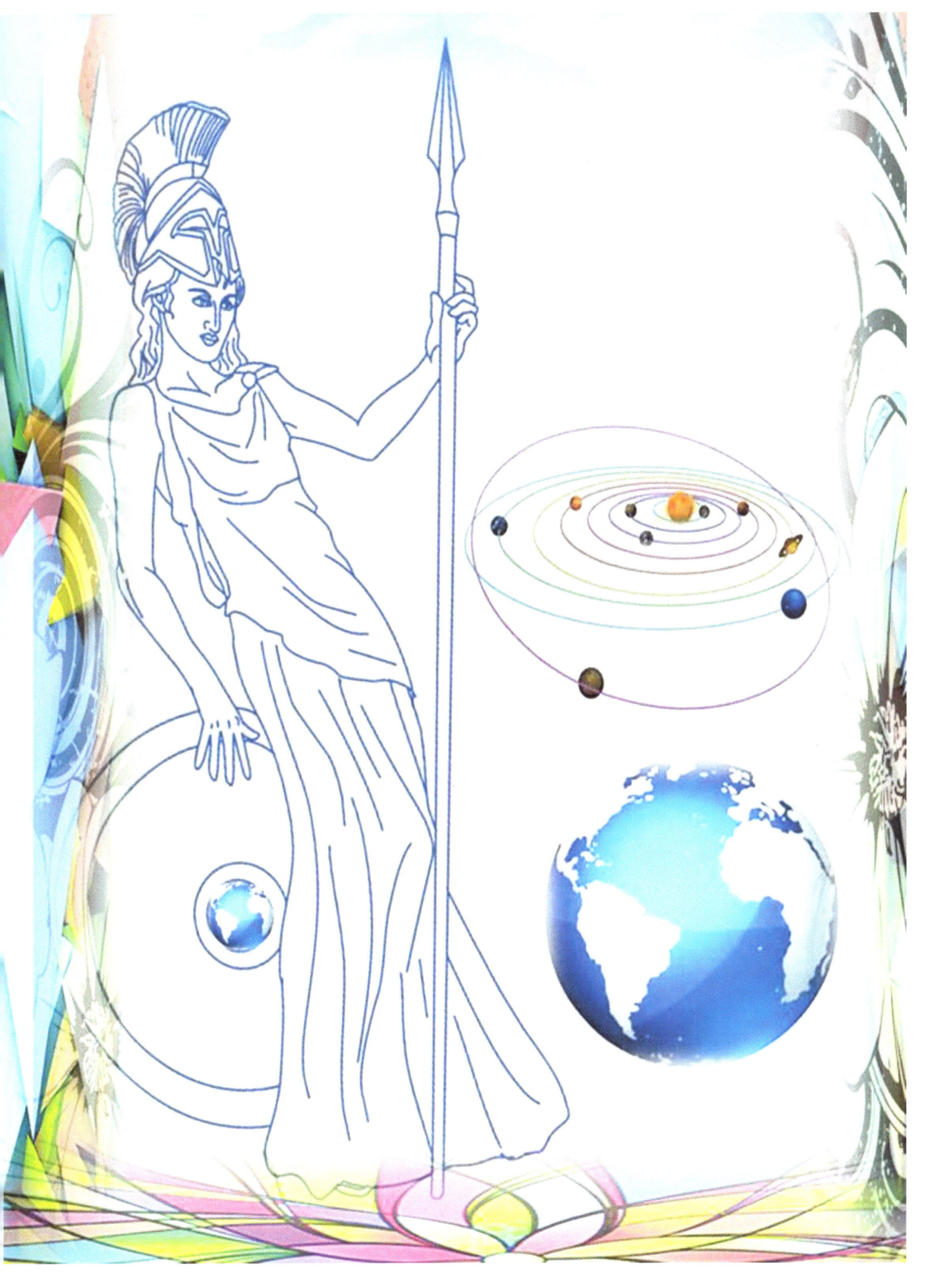

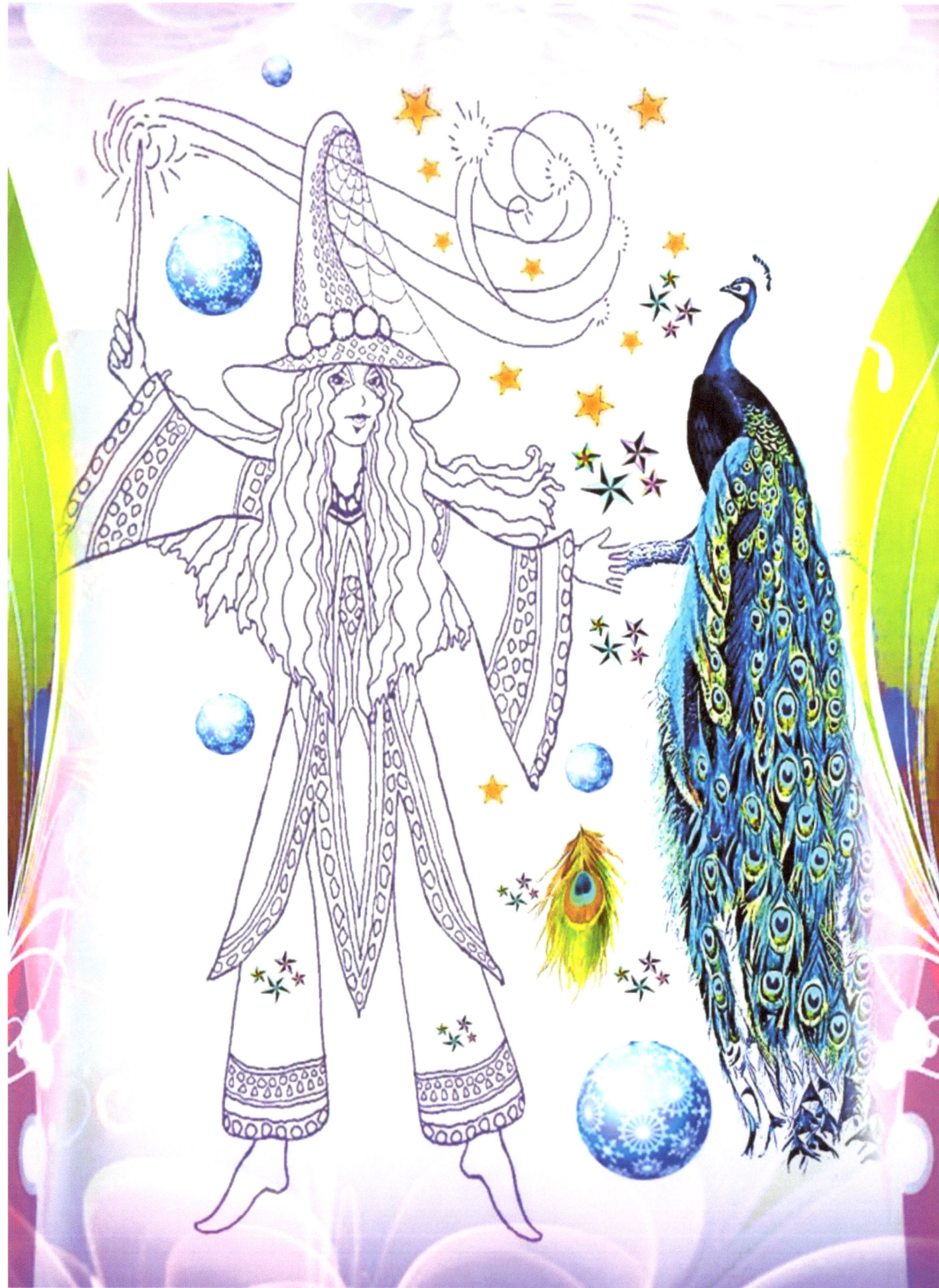

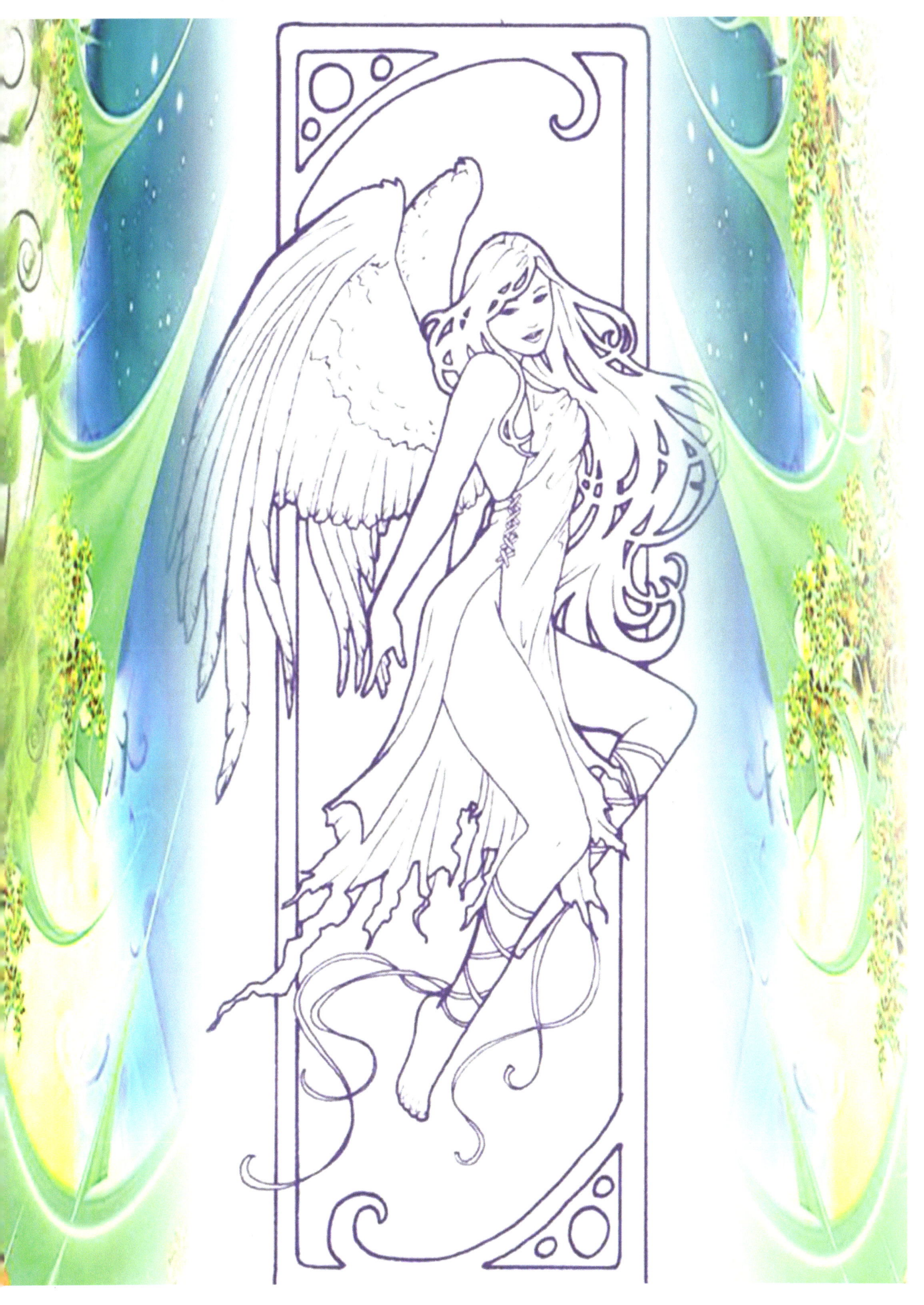

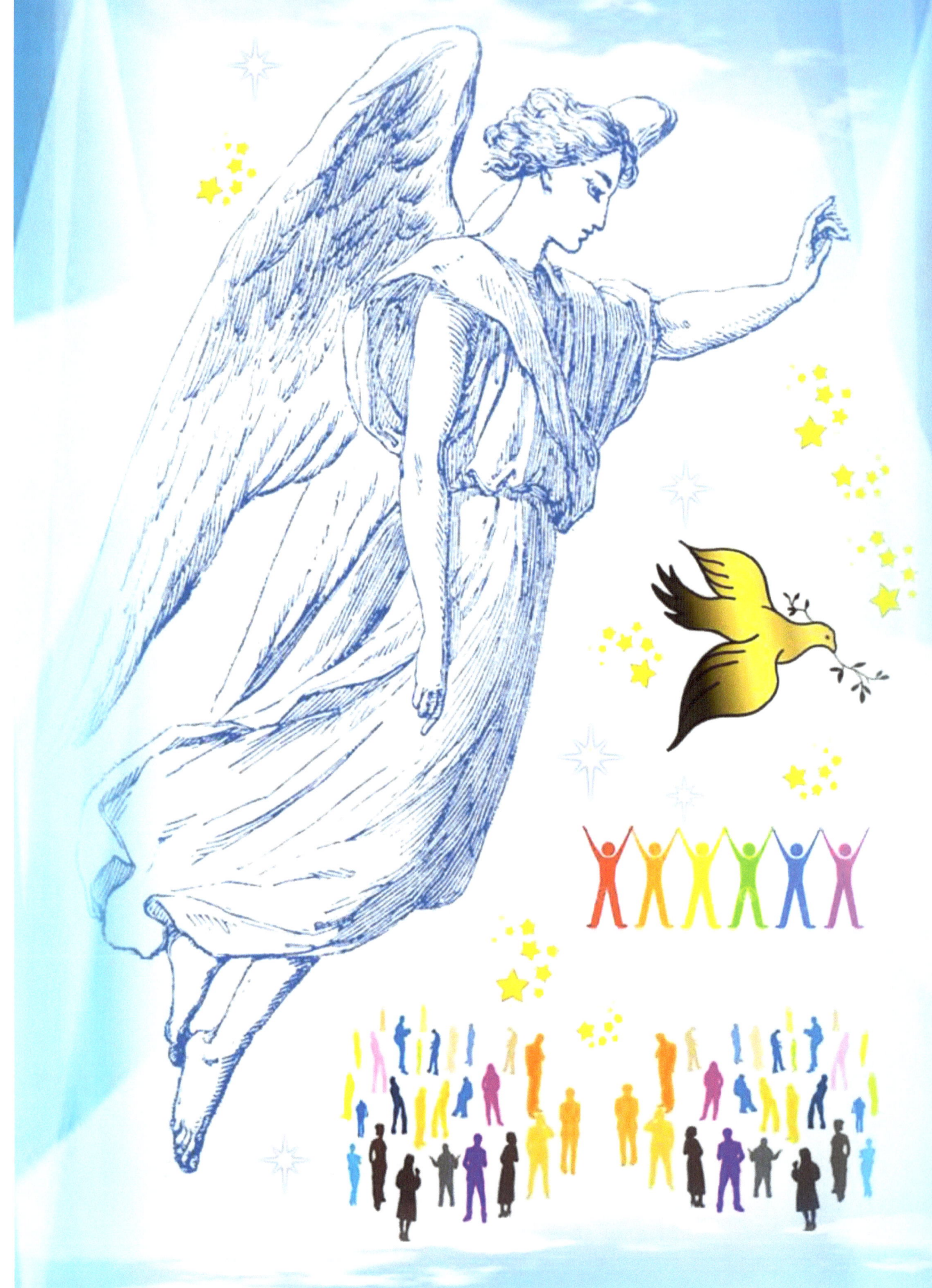

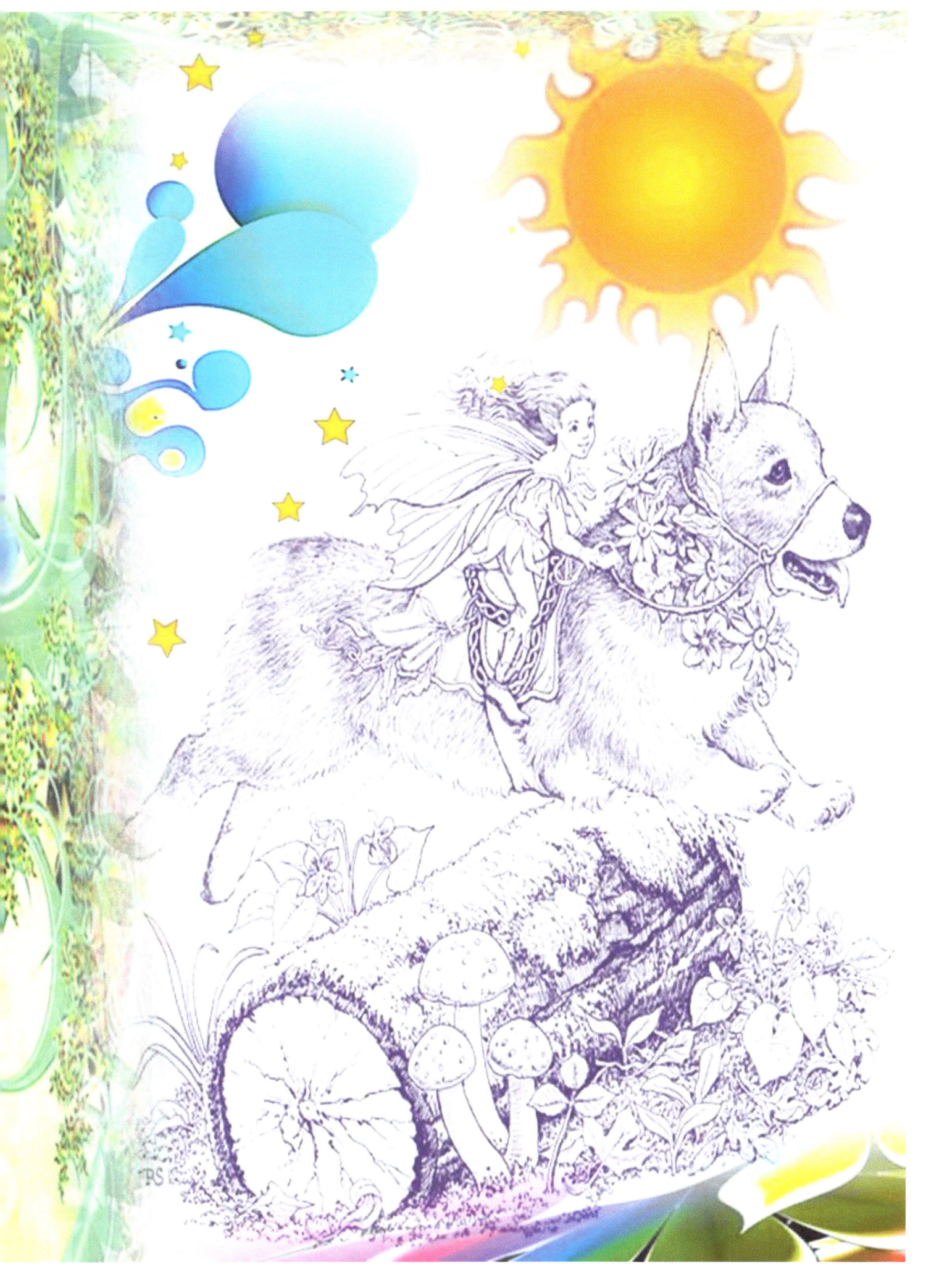

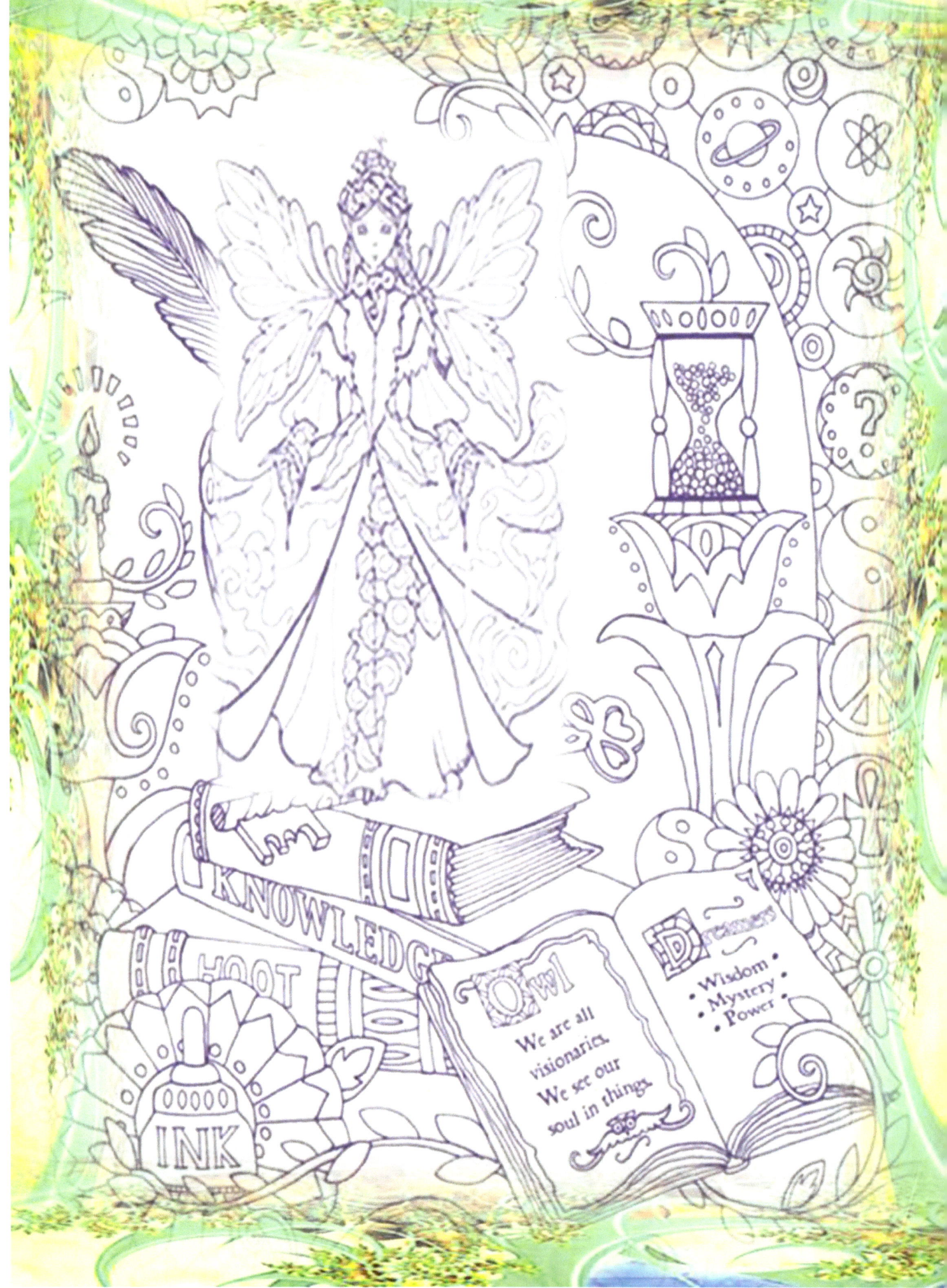

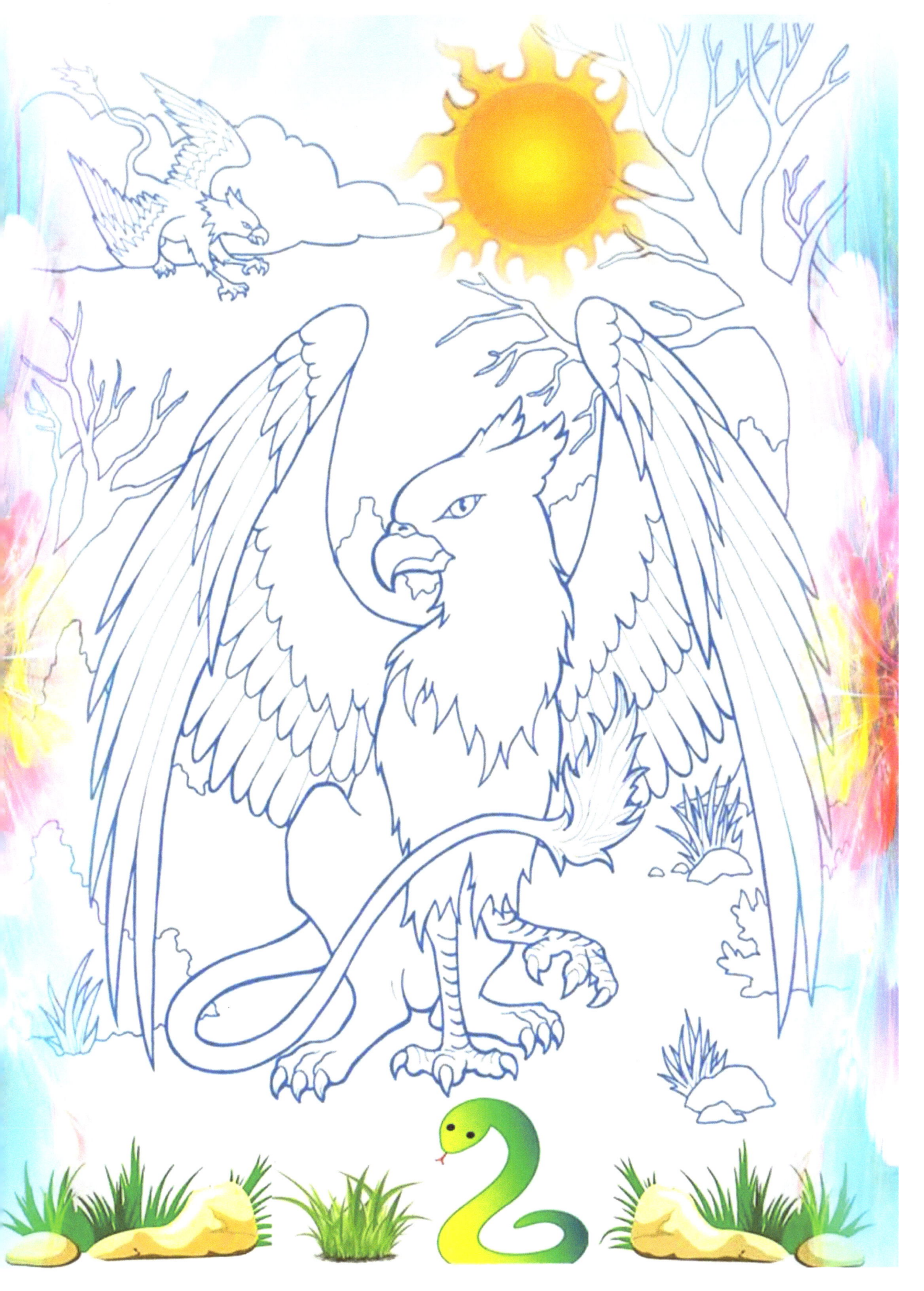

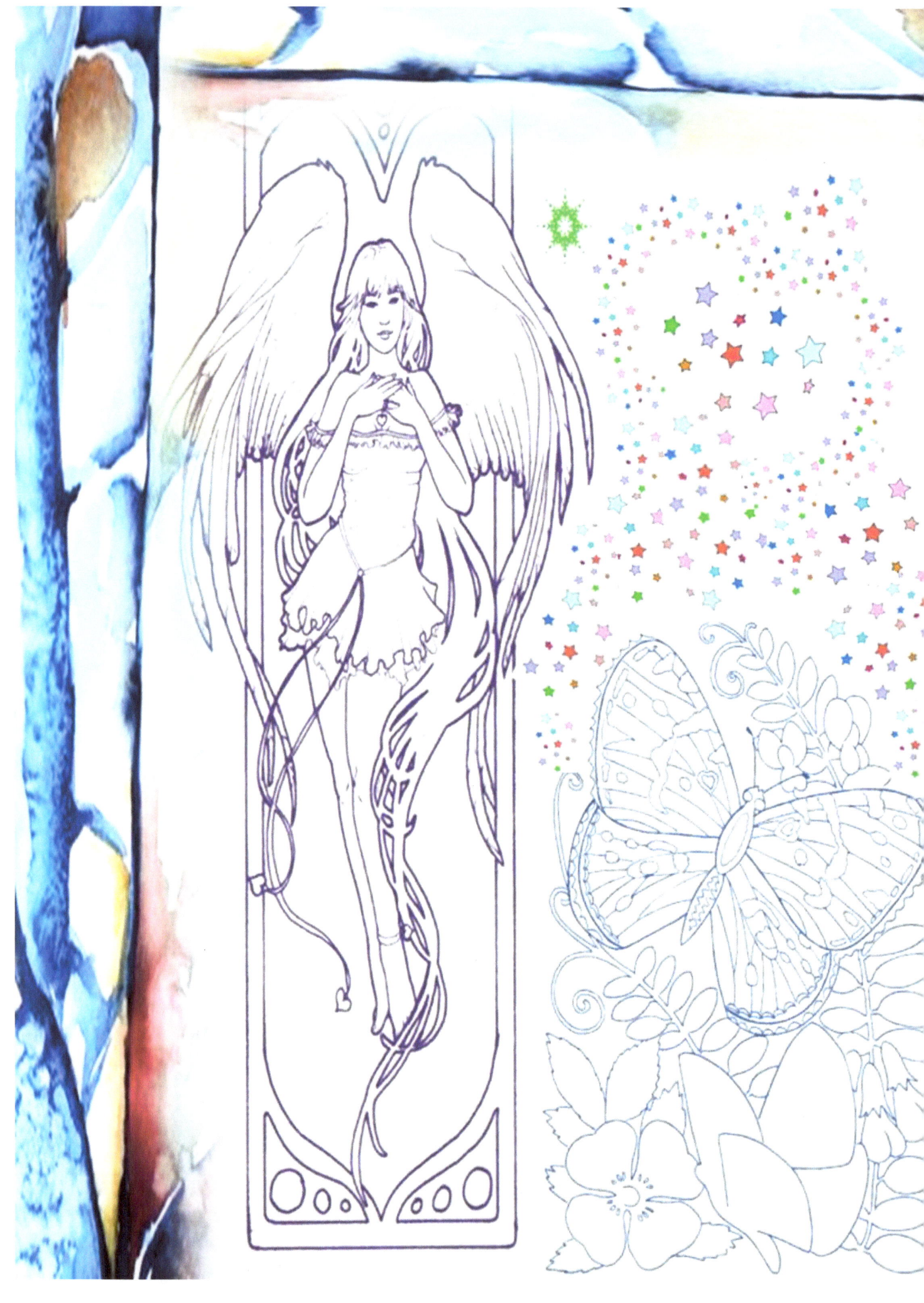

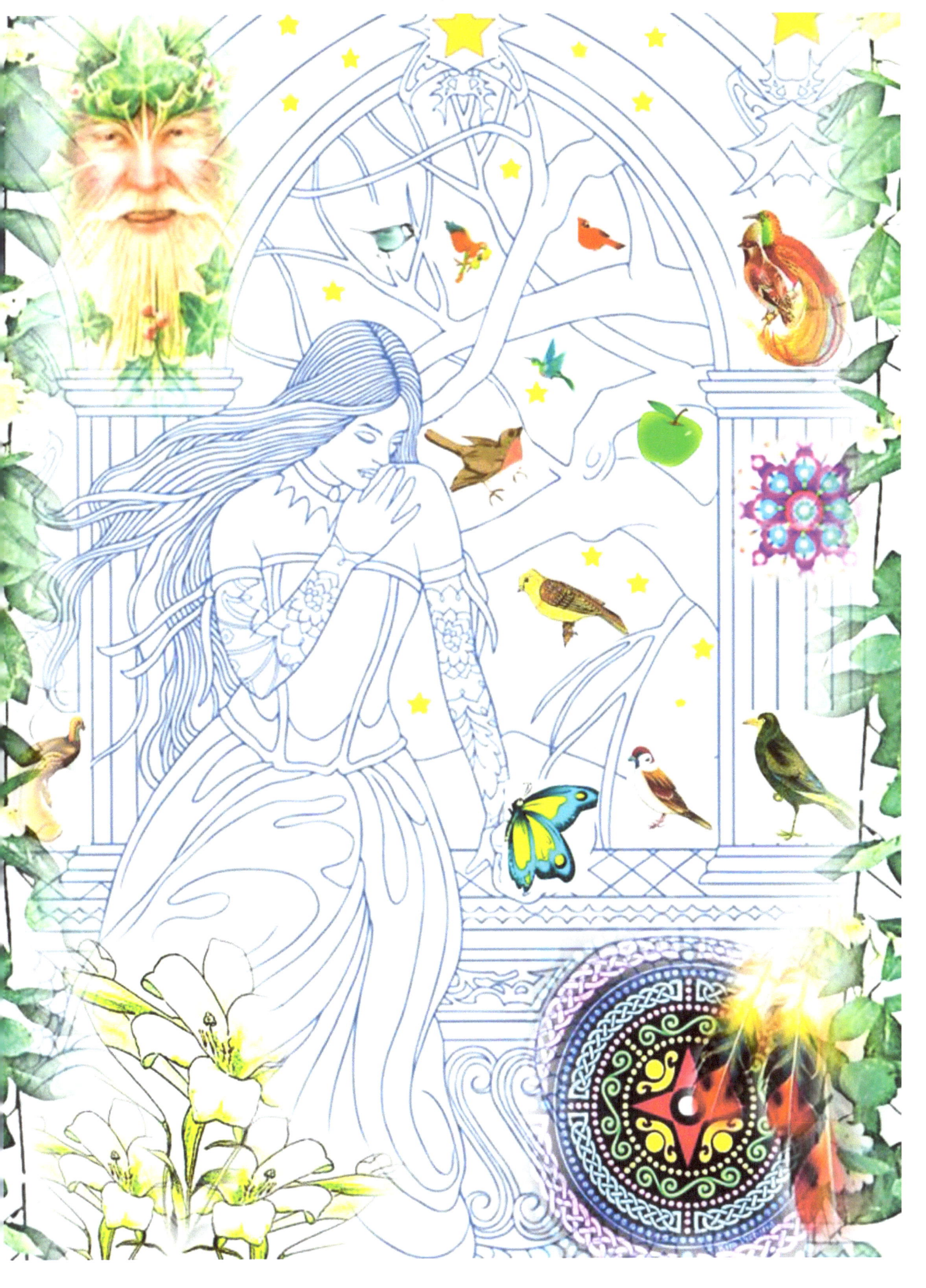

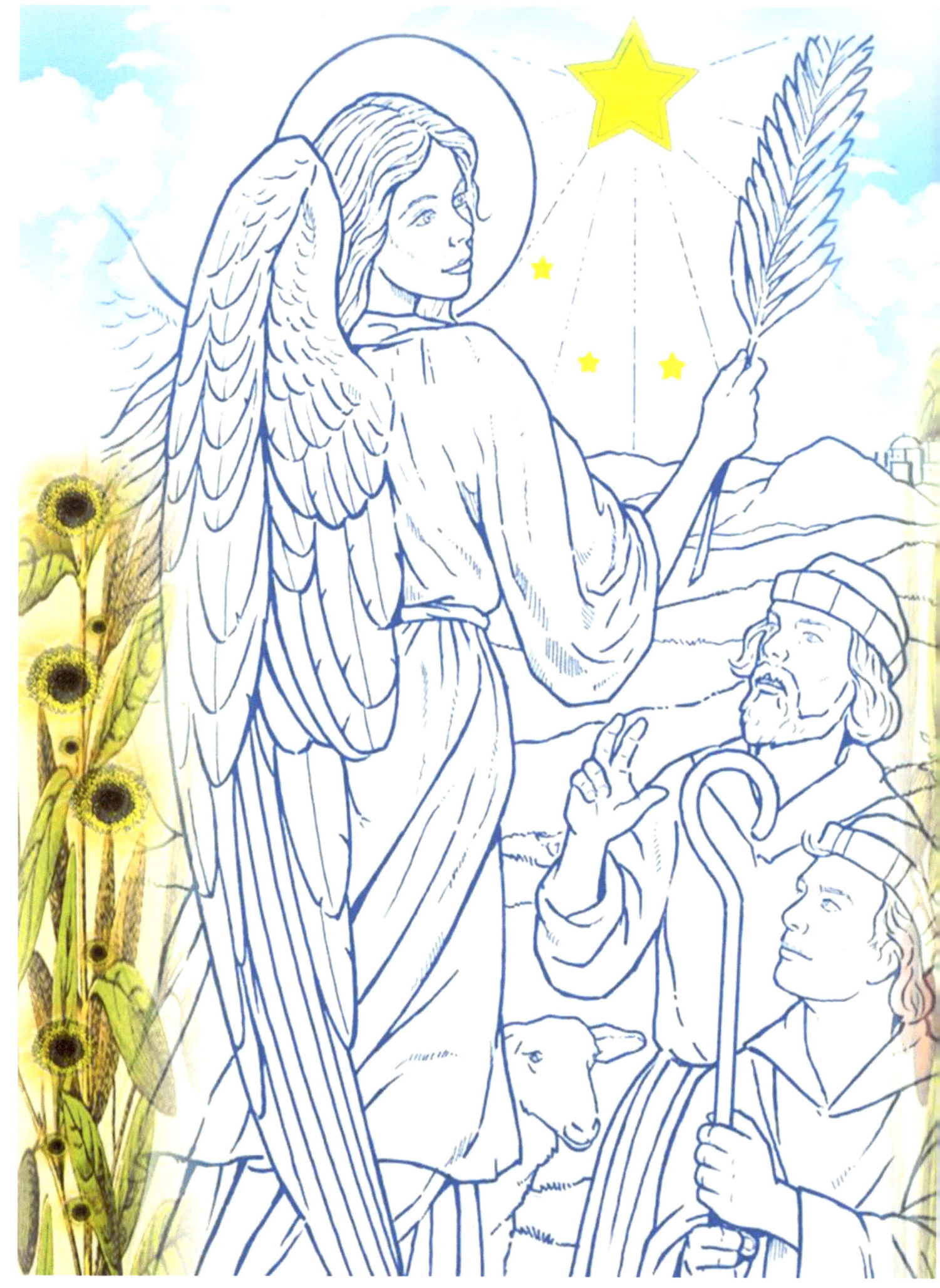

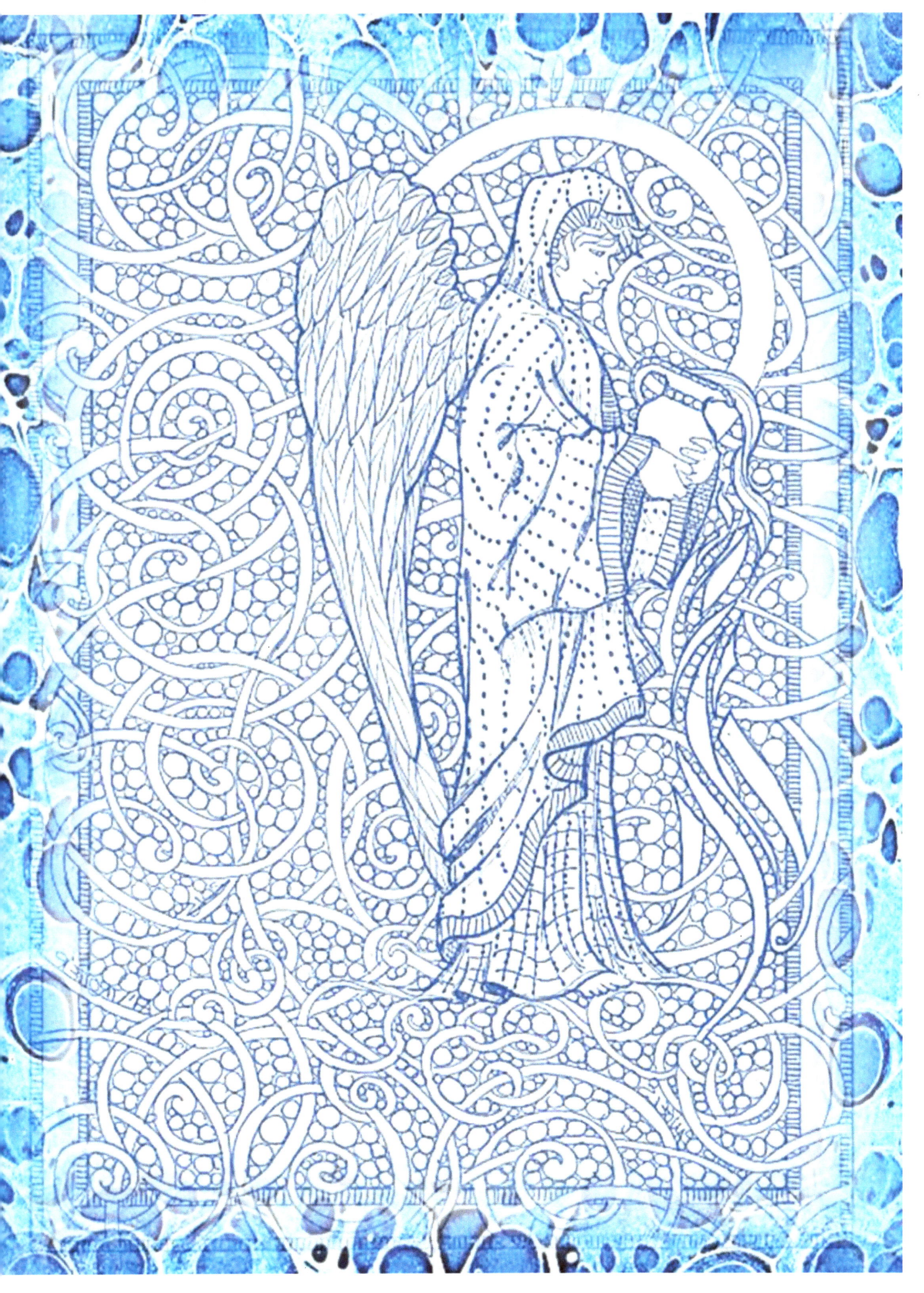

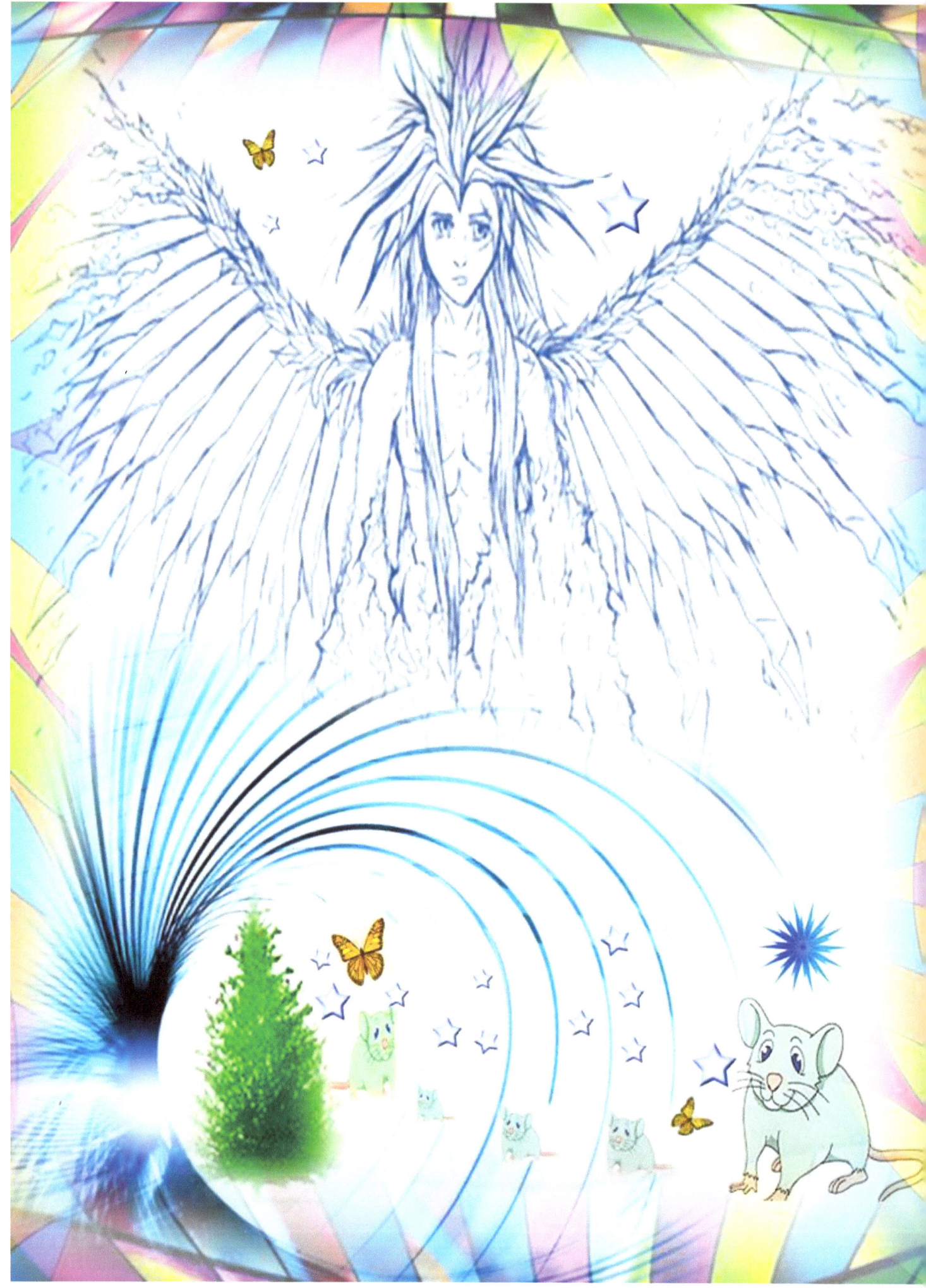

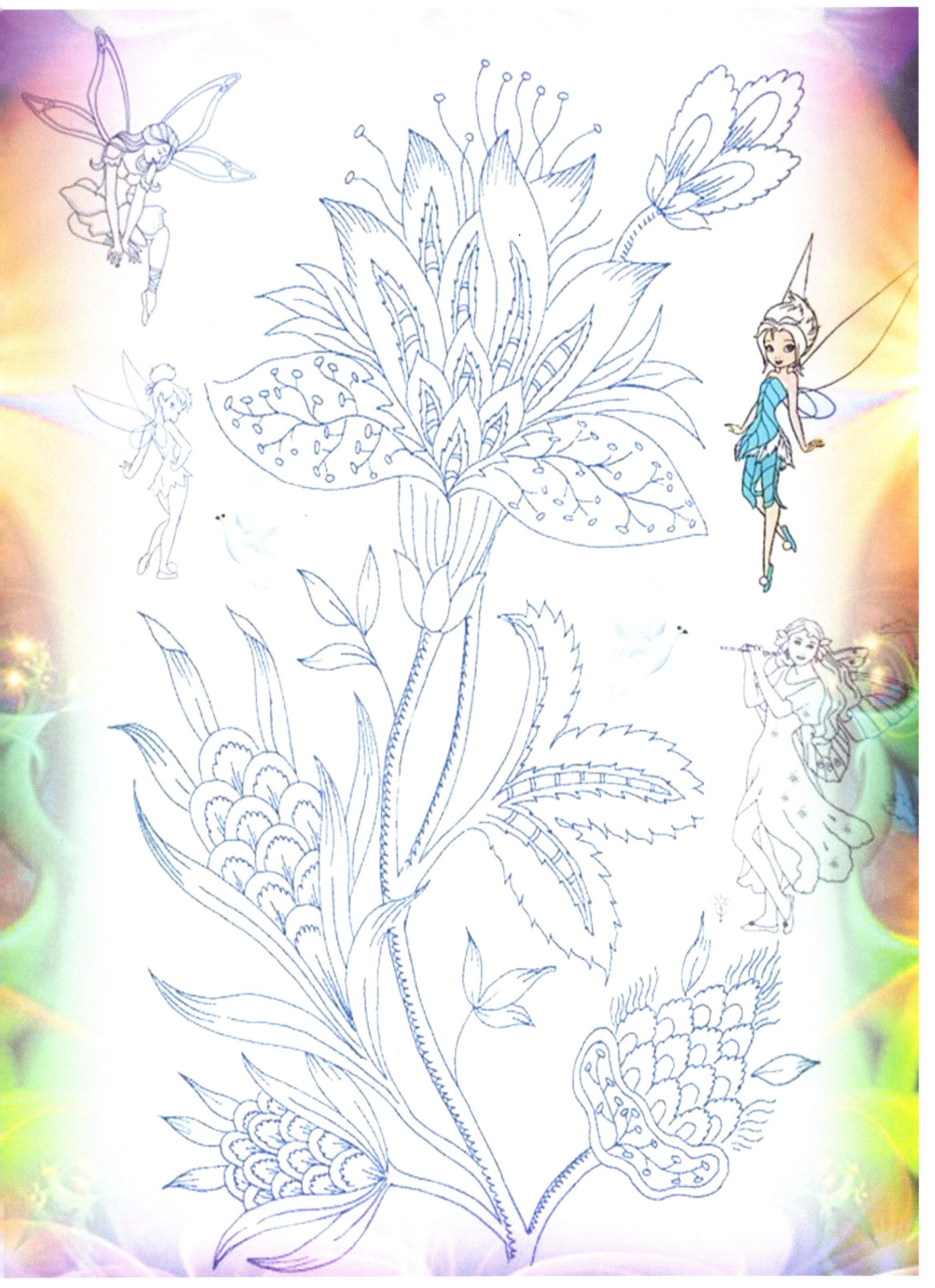

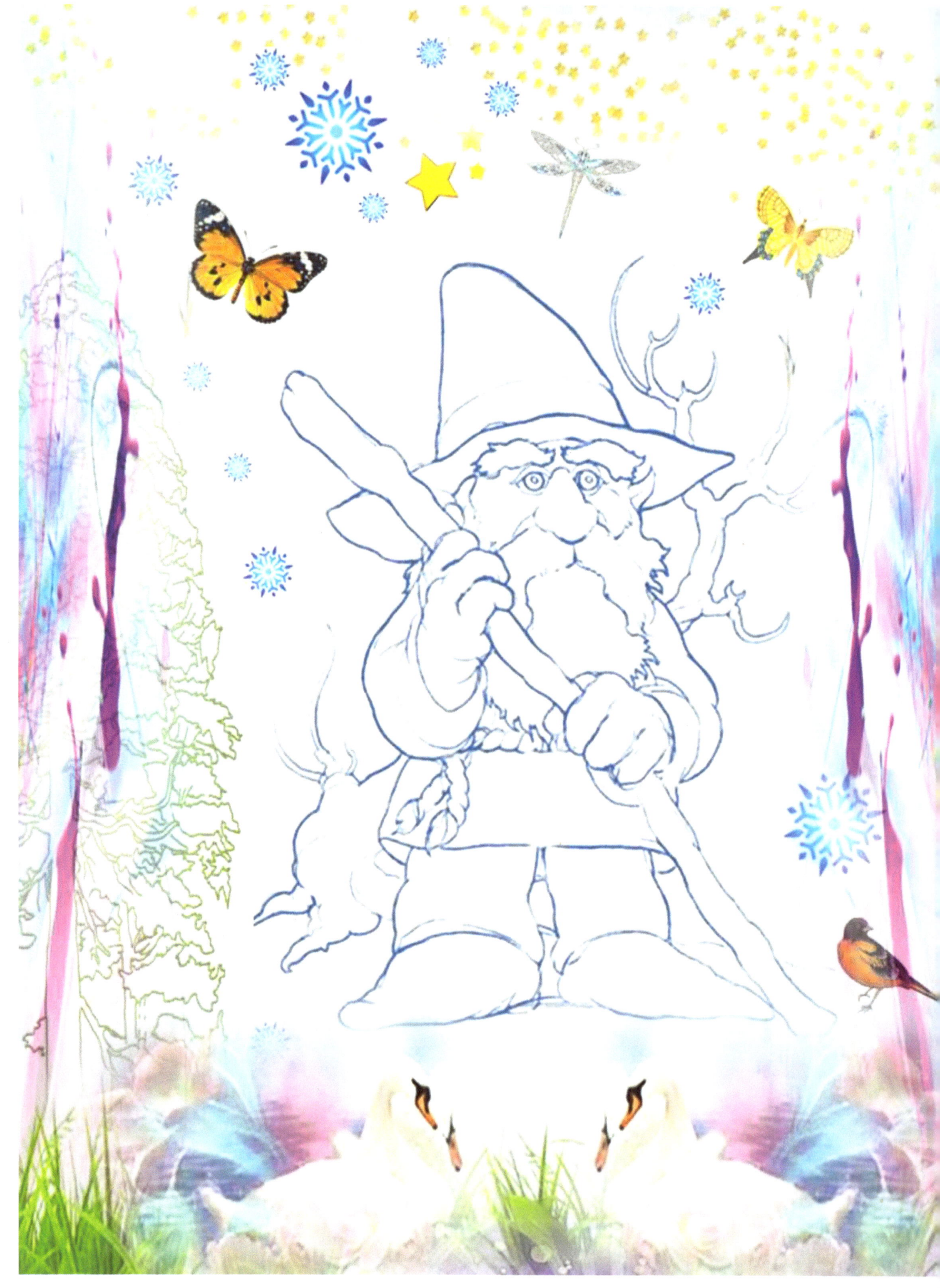

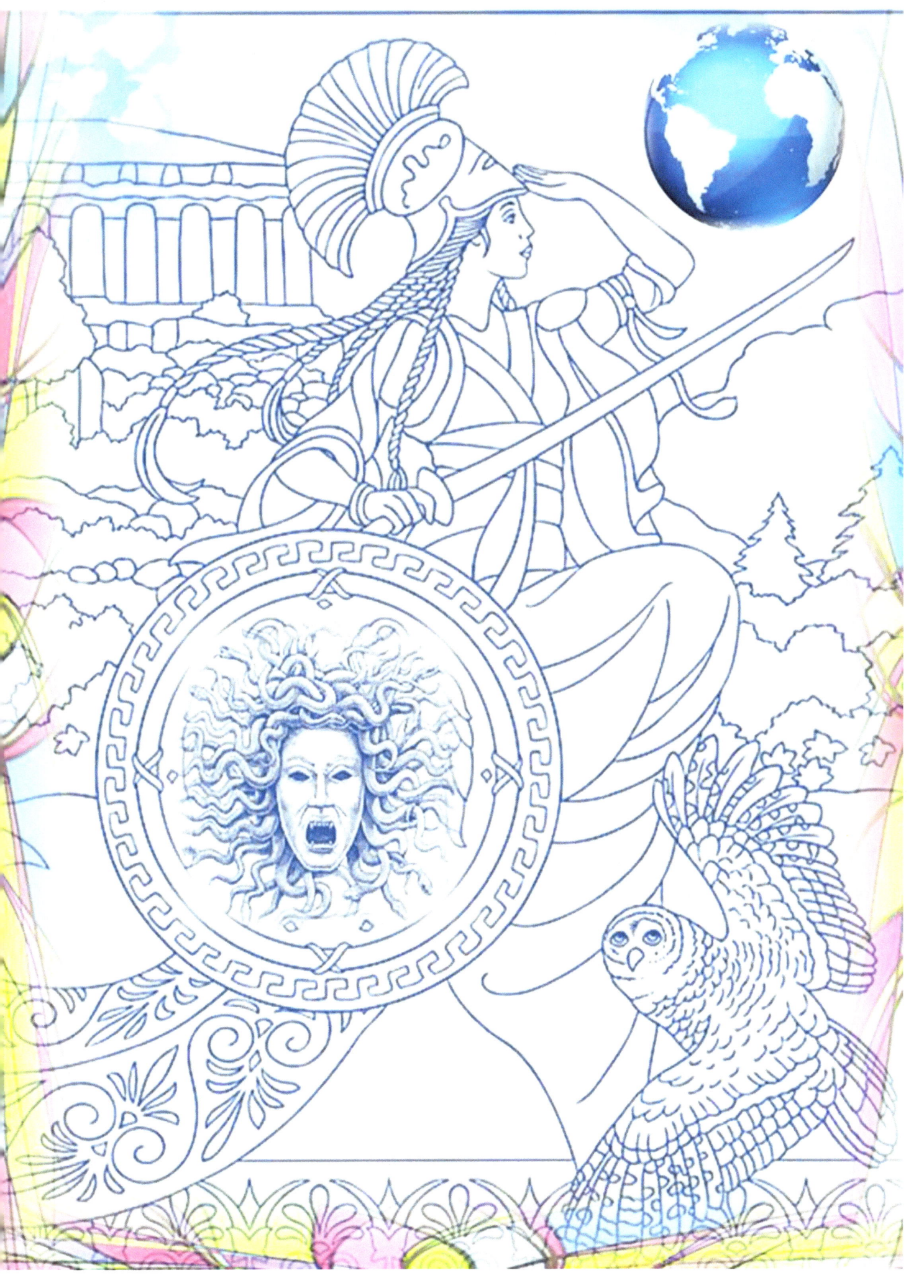

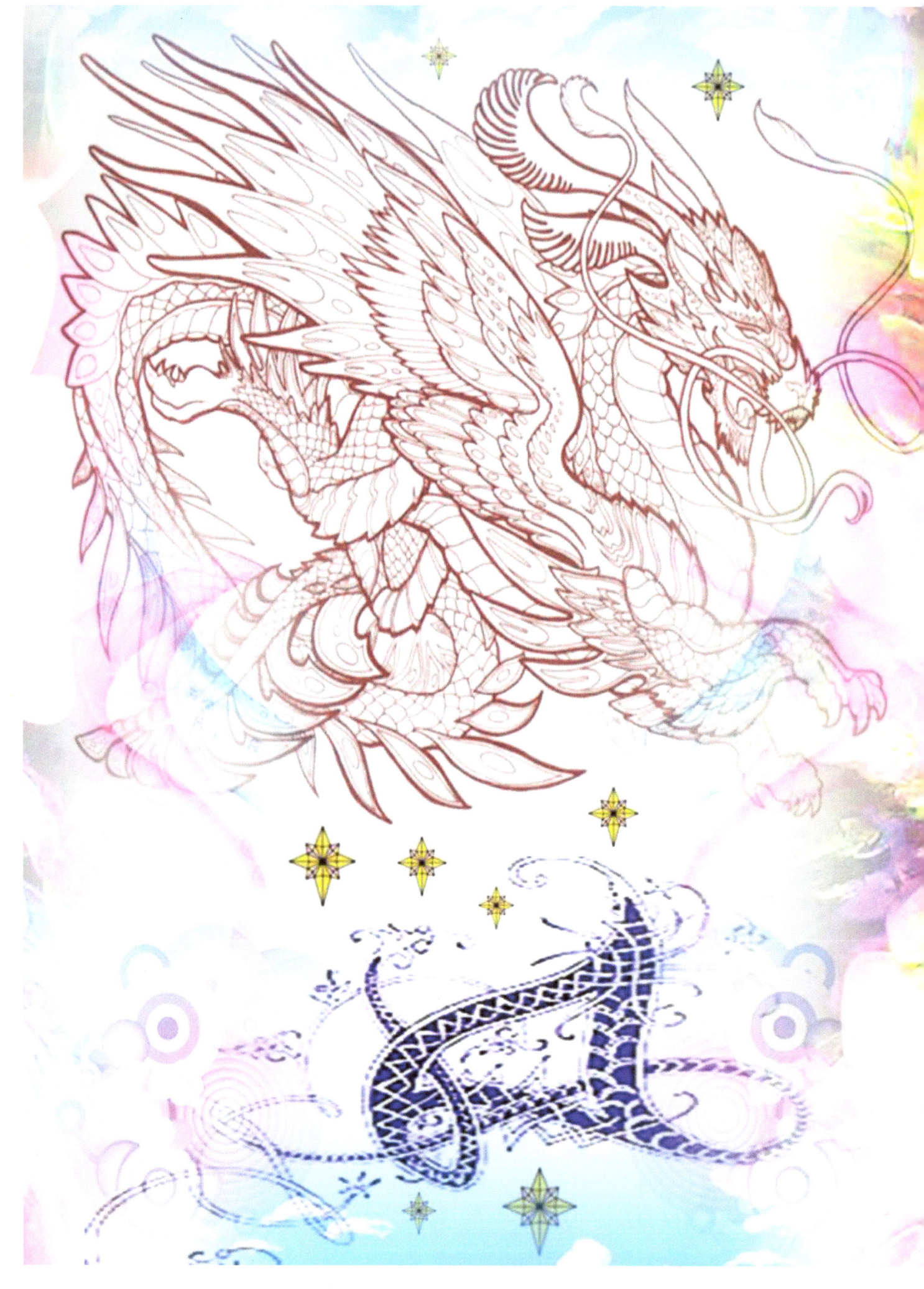

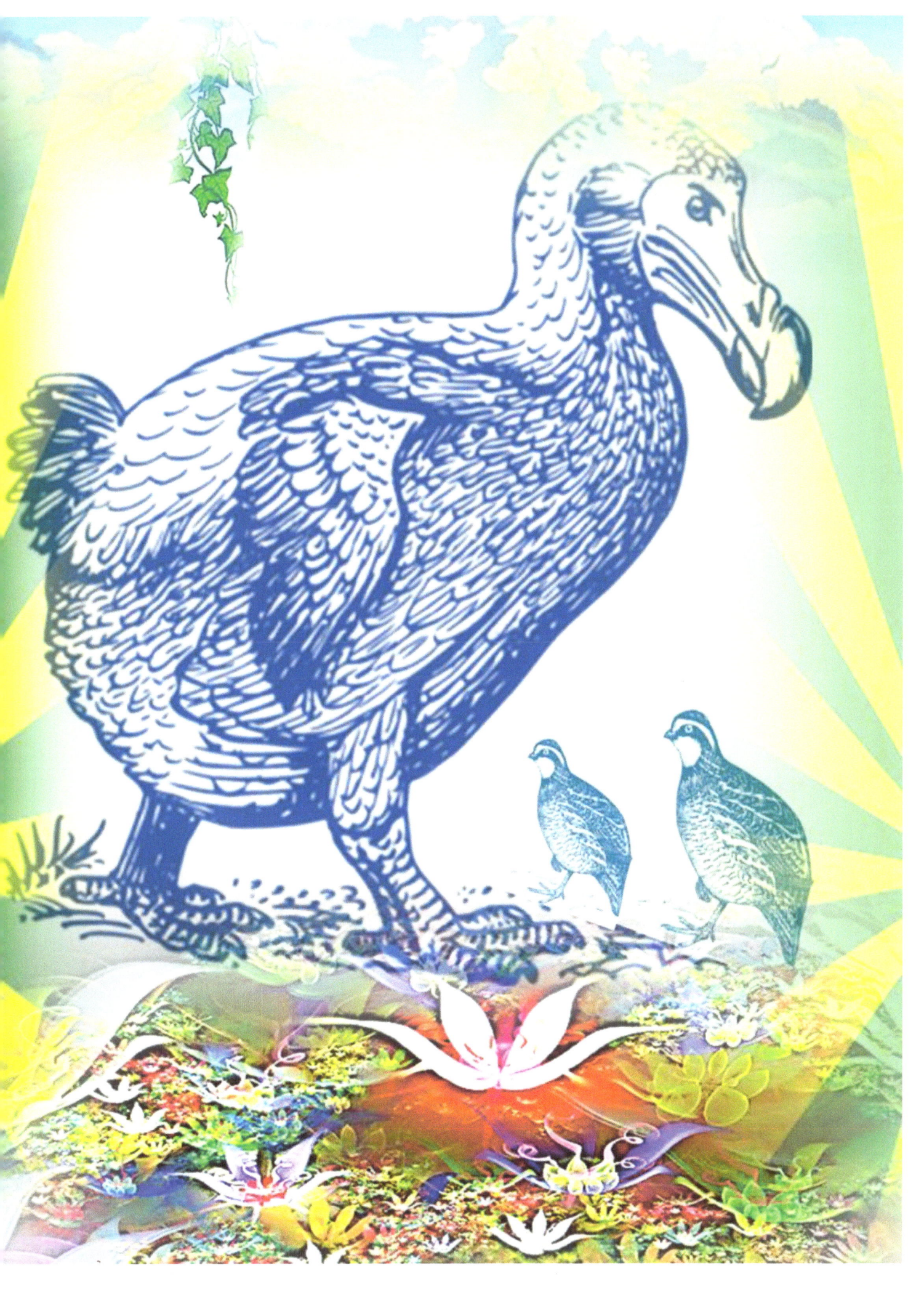

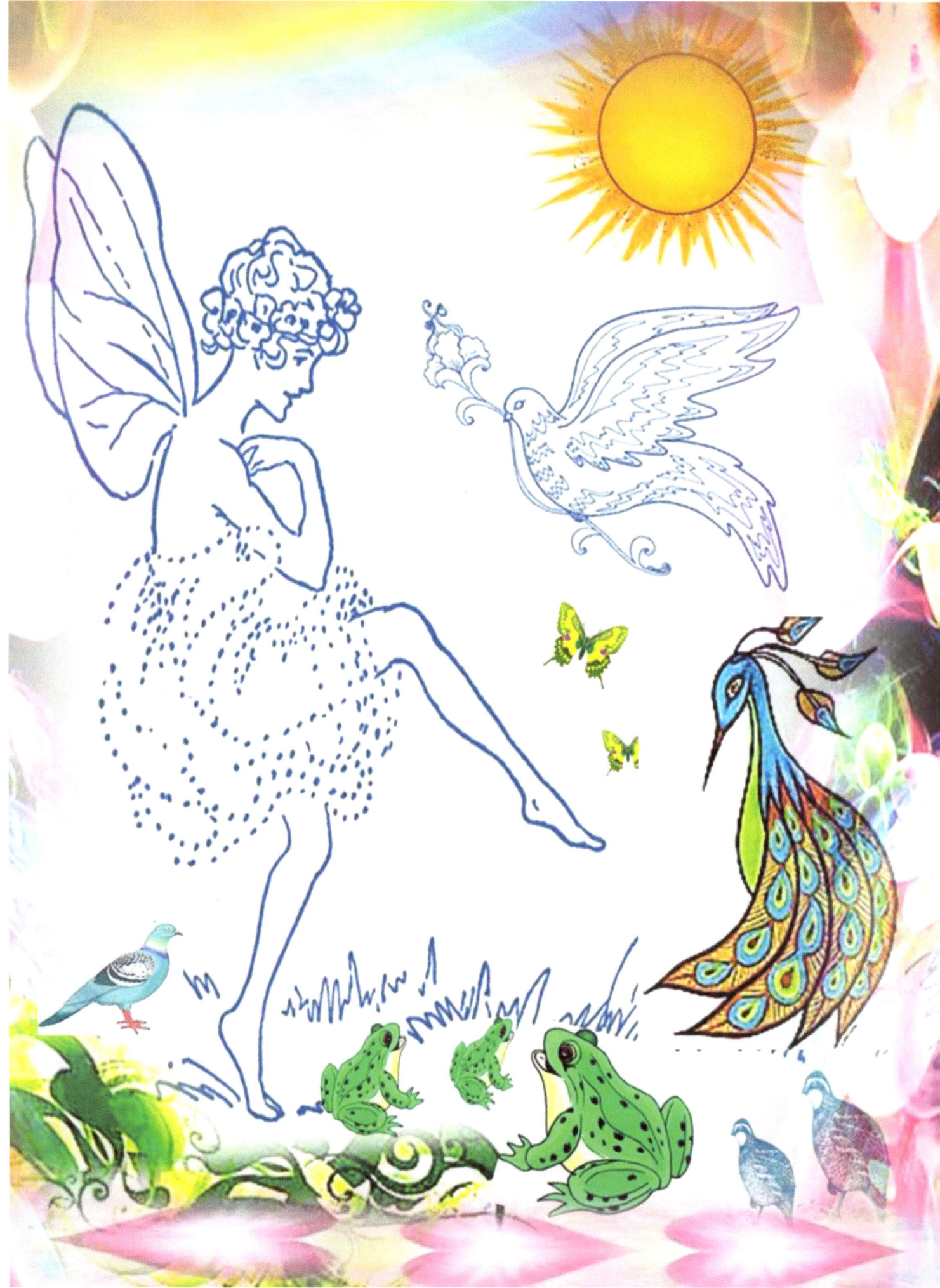

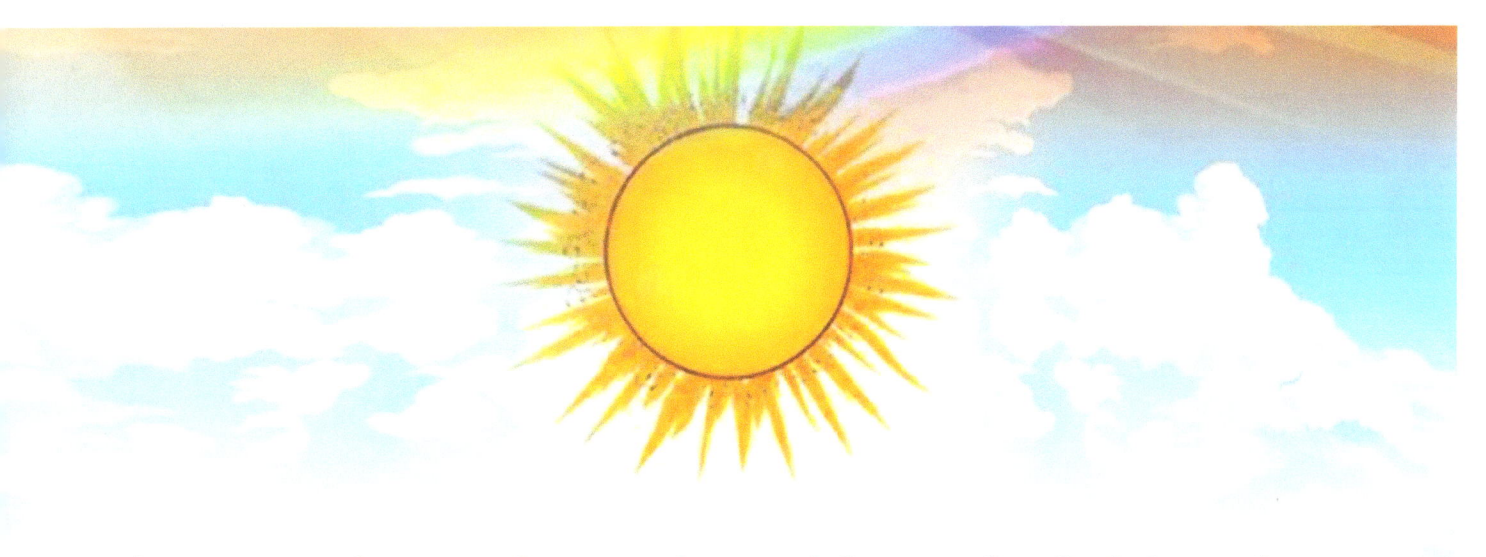

There are legends in The Bible and of olden days.

That Magical Beings are real in so many ways.

They were born of angels and humans, long ago.

Their presence was a mixture of joy...and sorrow.

Legend has it, they ate their way out of the womb!

Giants and more they were, magical beings; I presume!

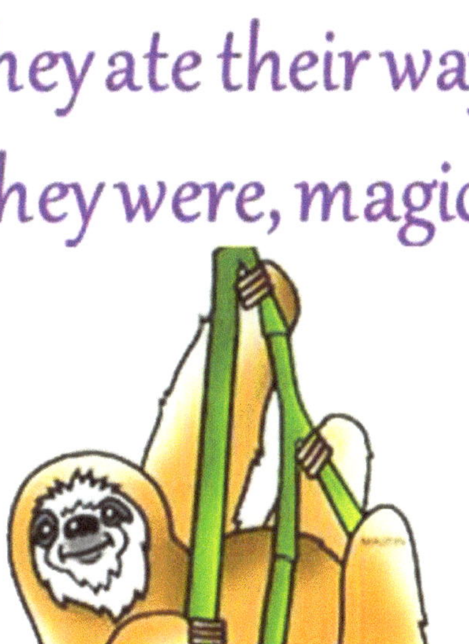

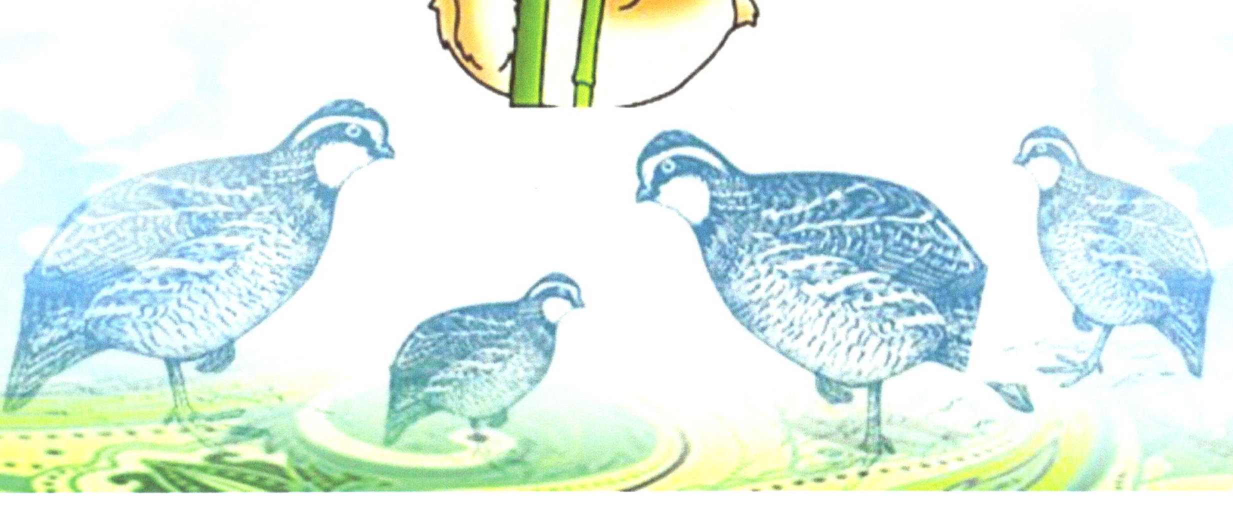

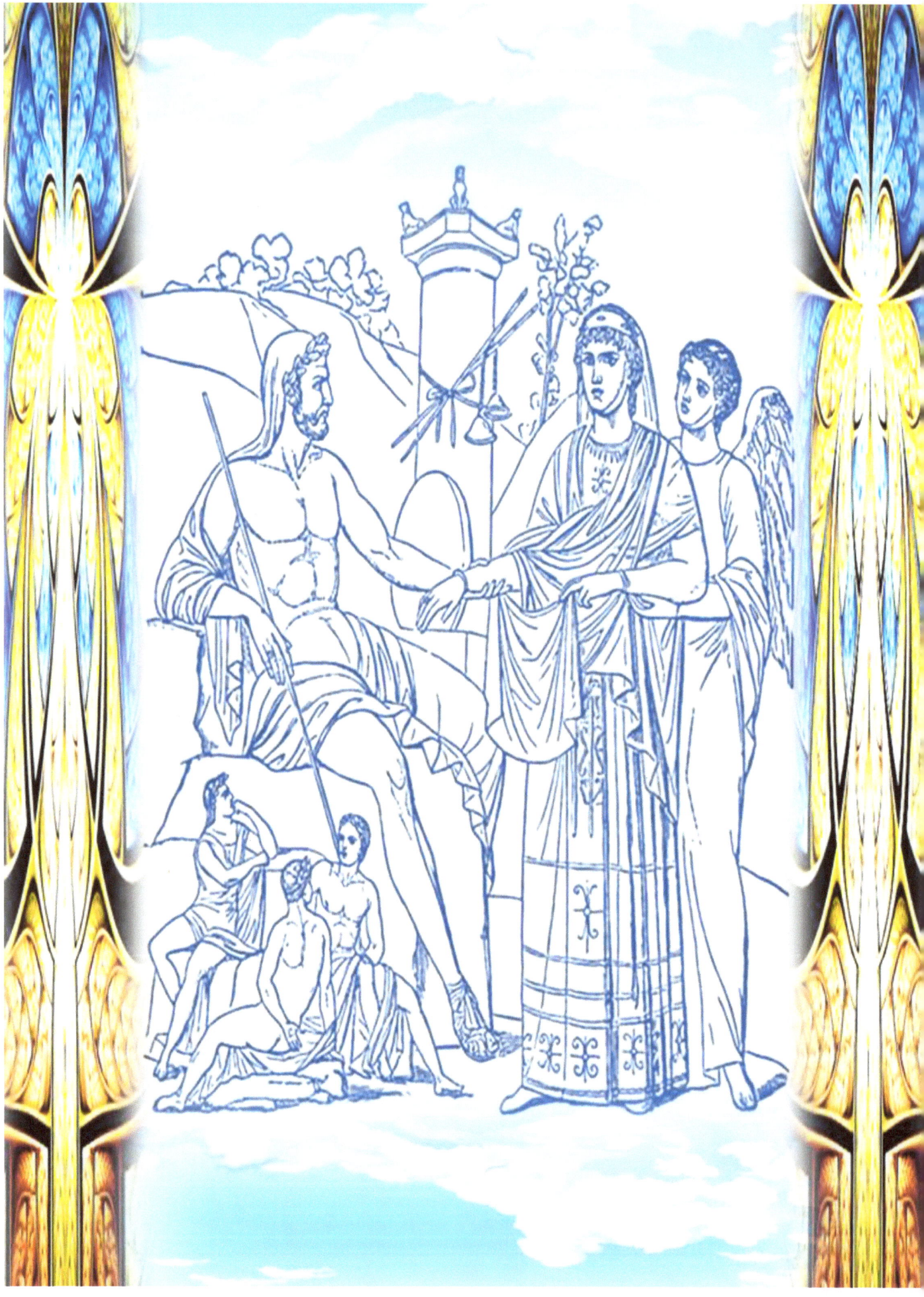

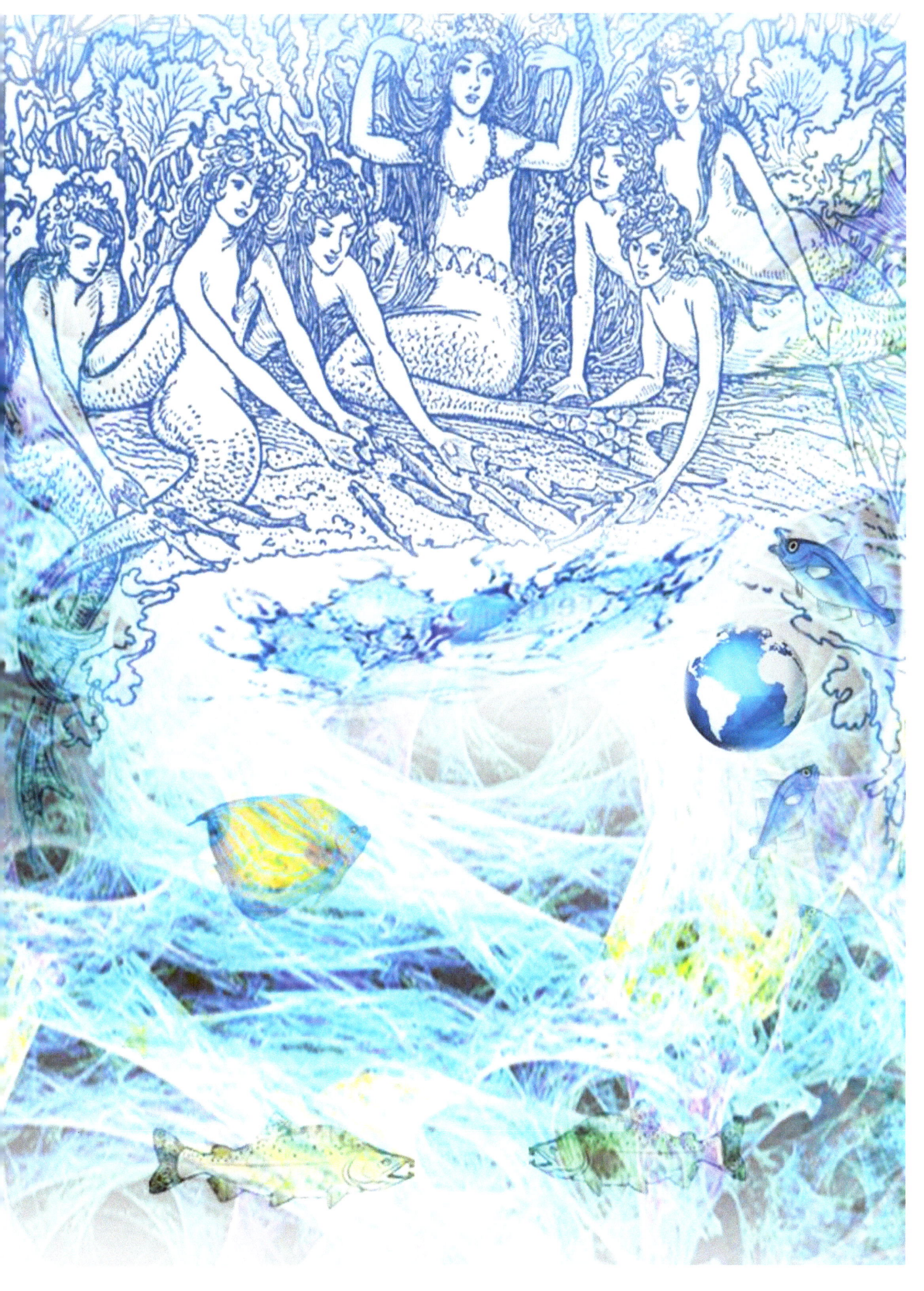

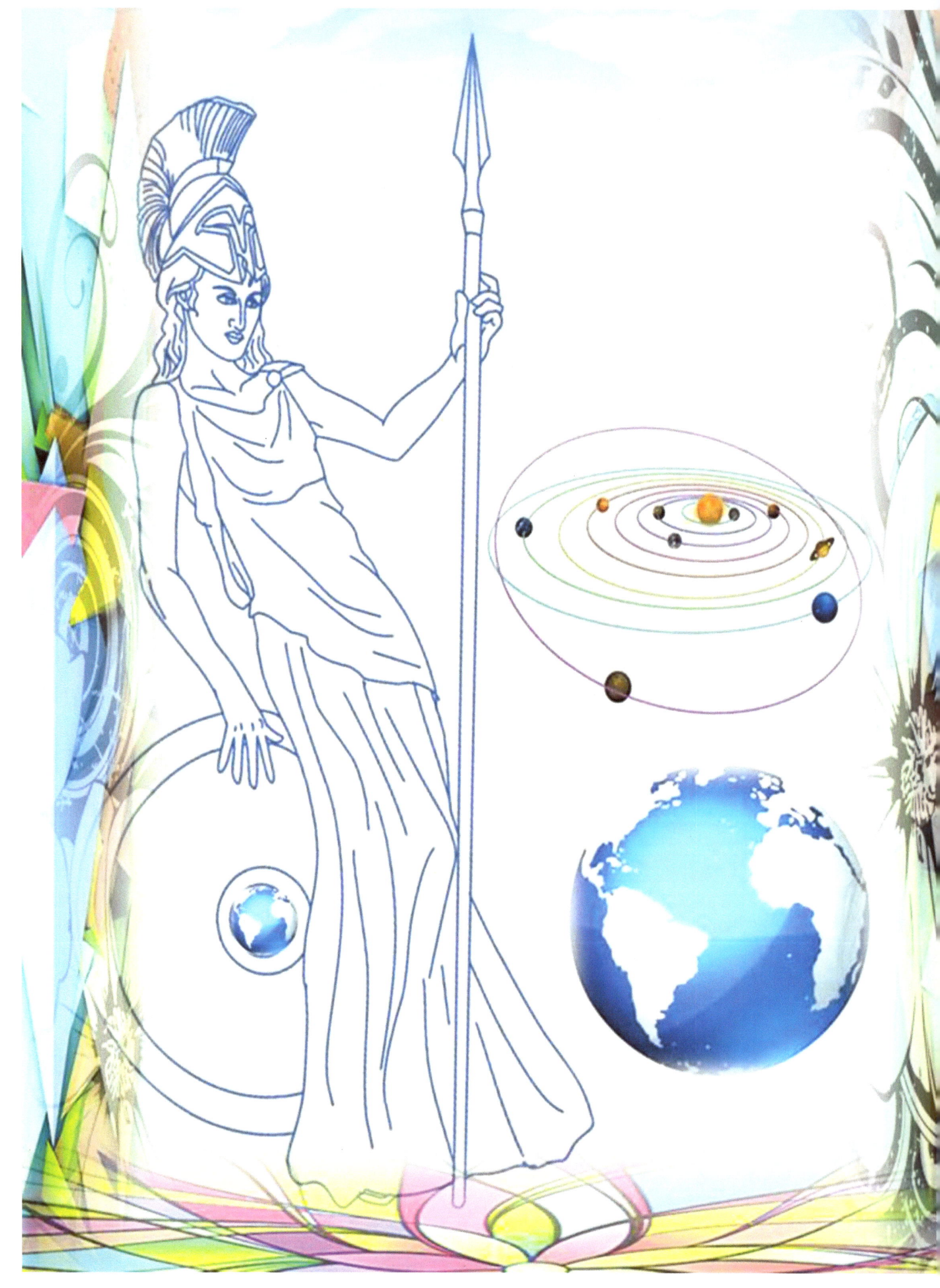

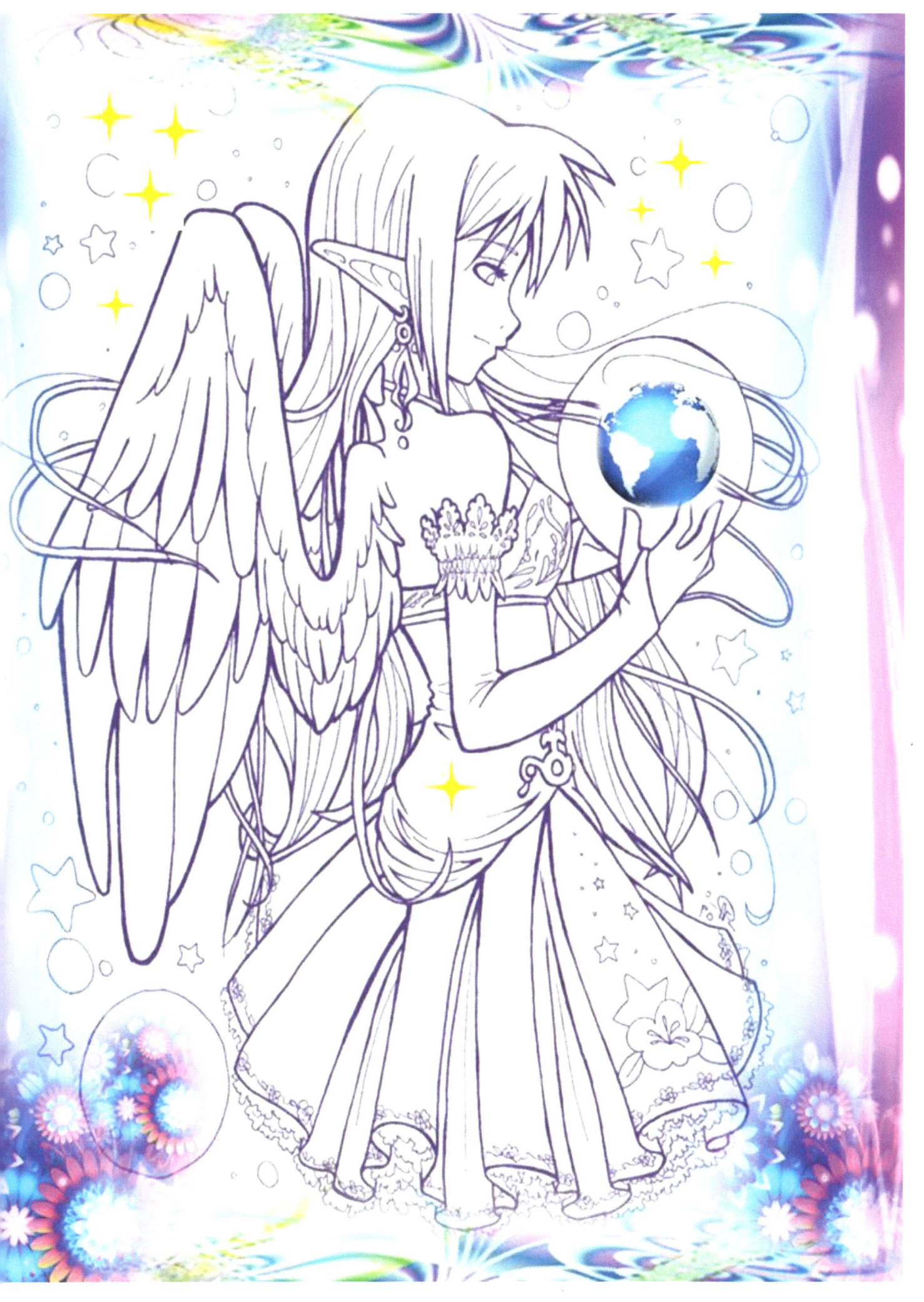

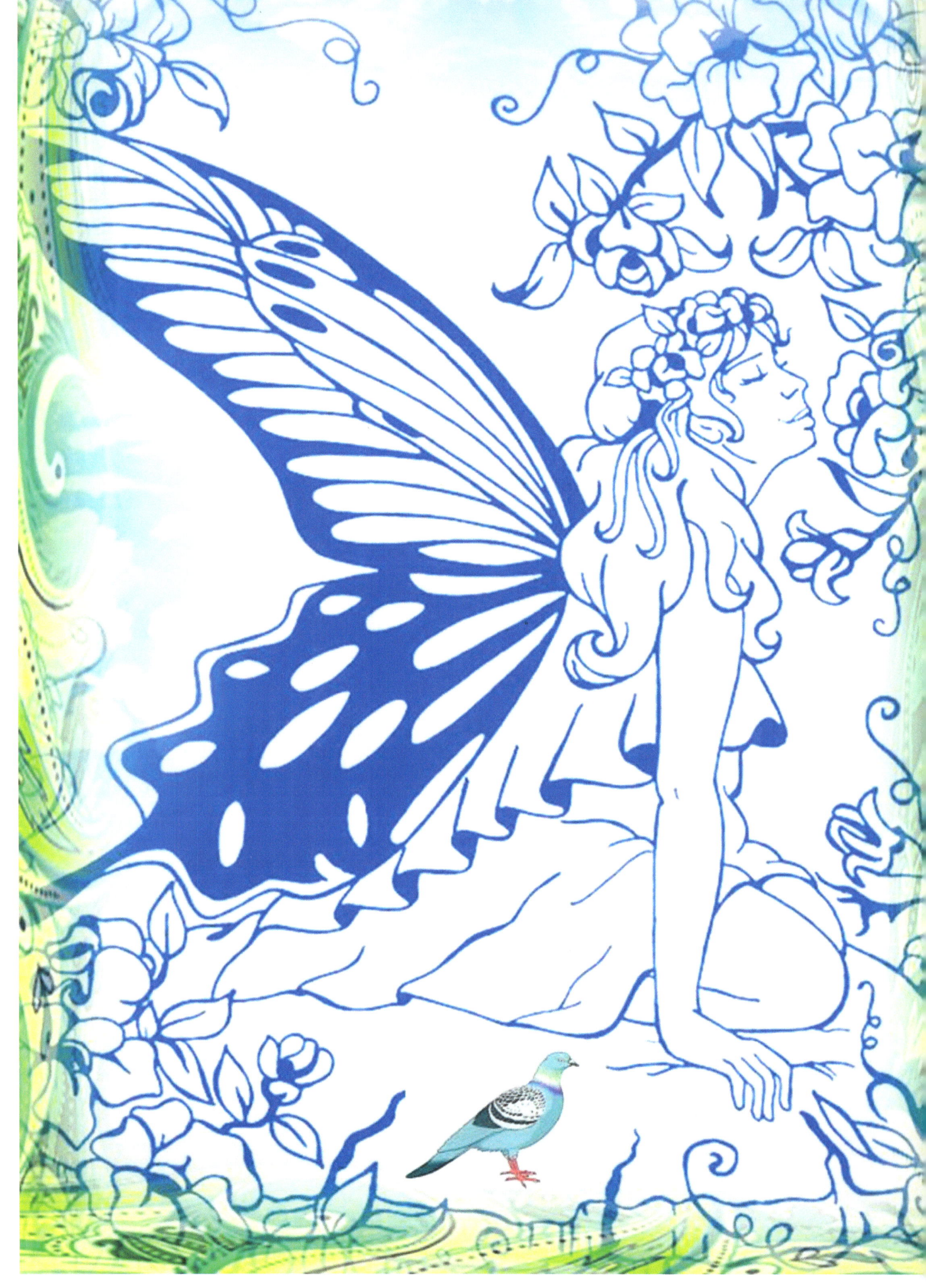

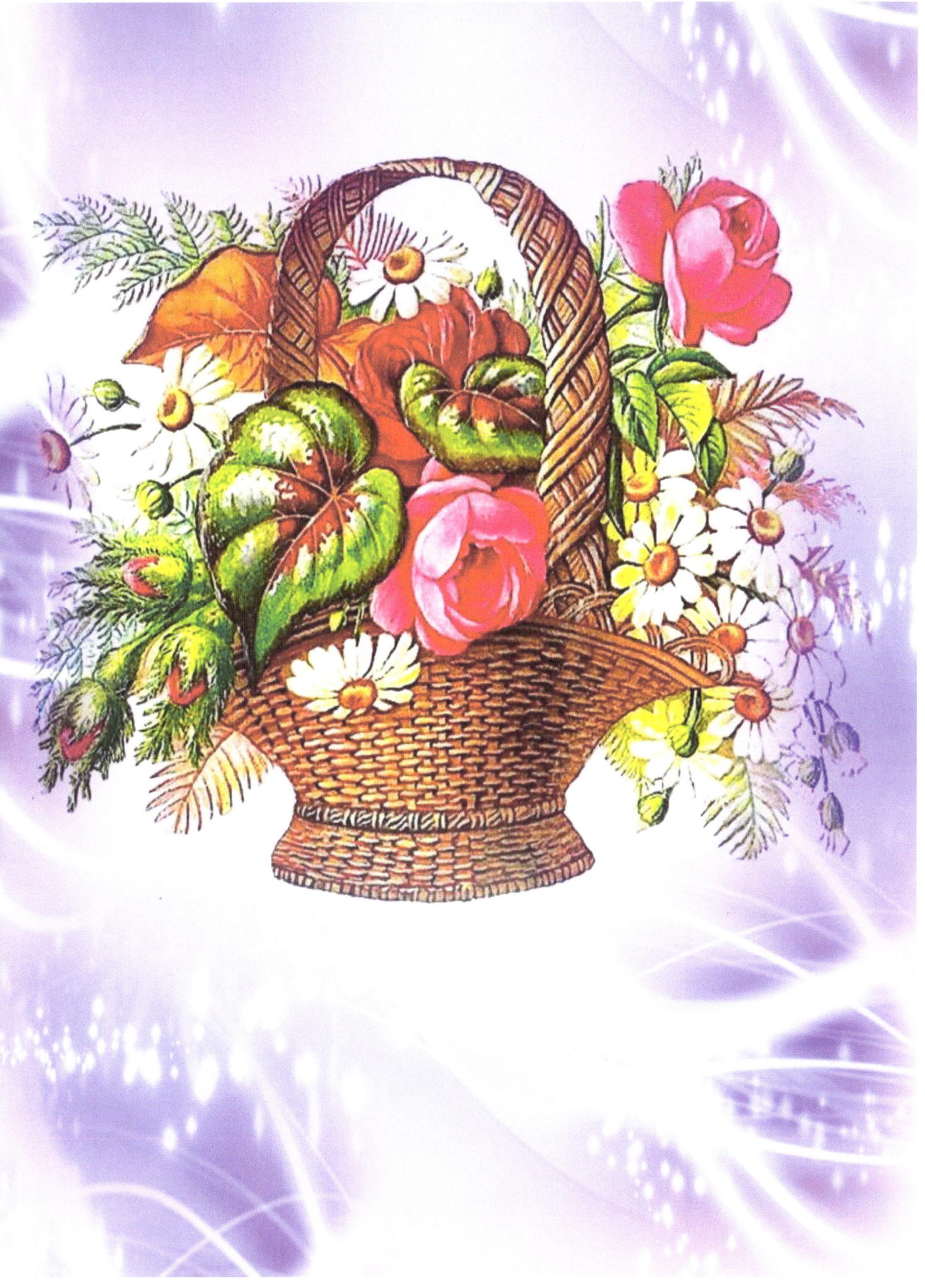

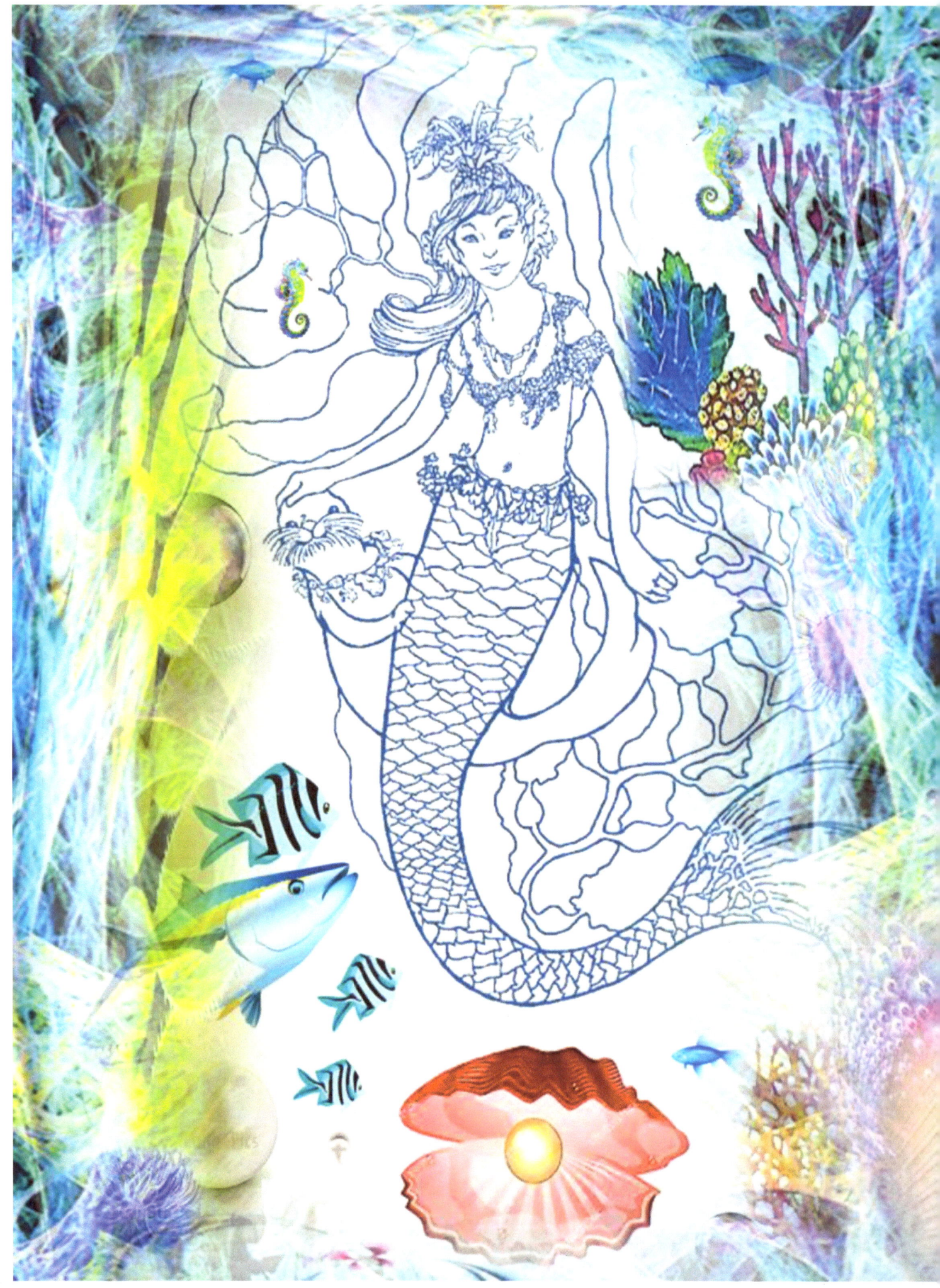

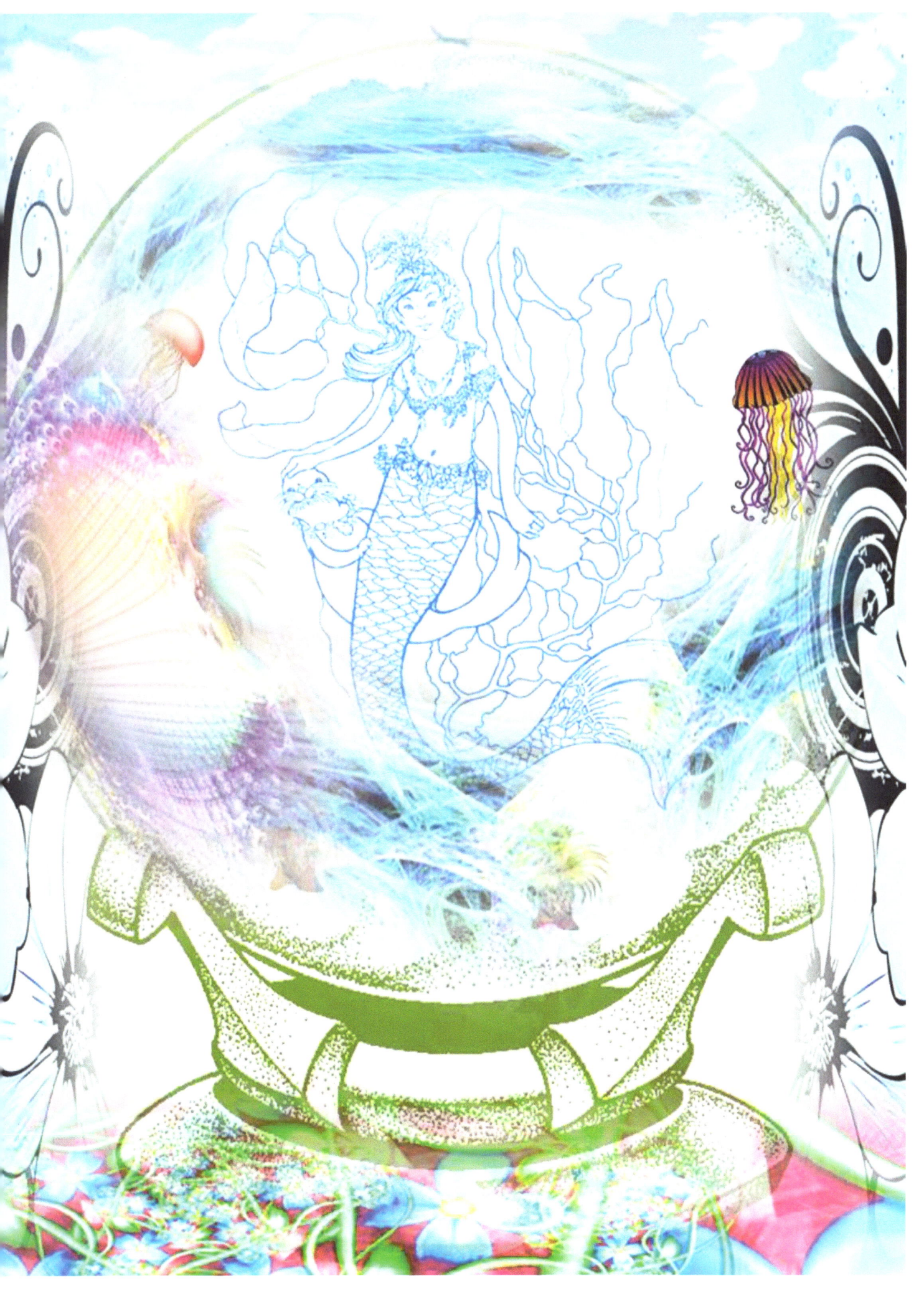

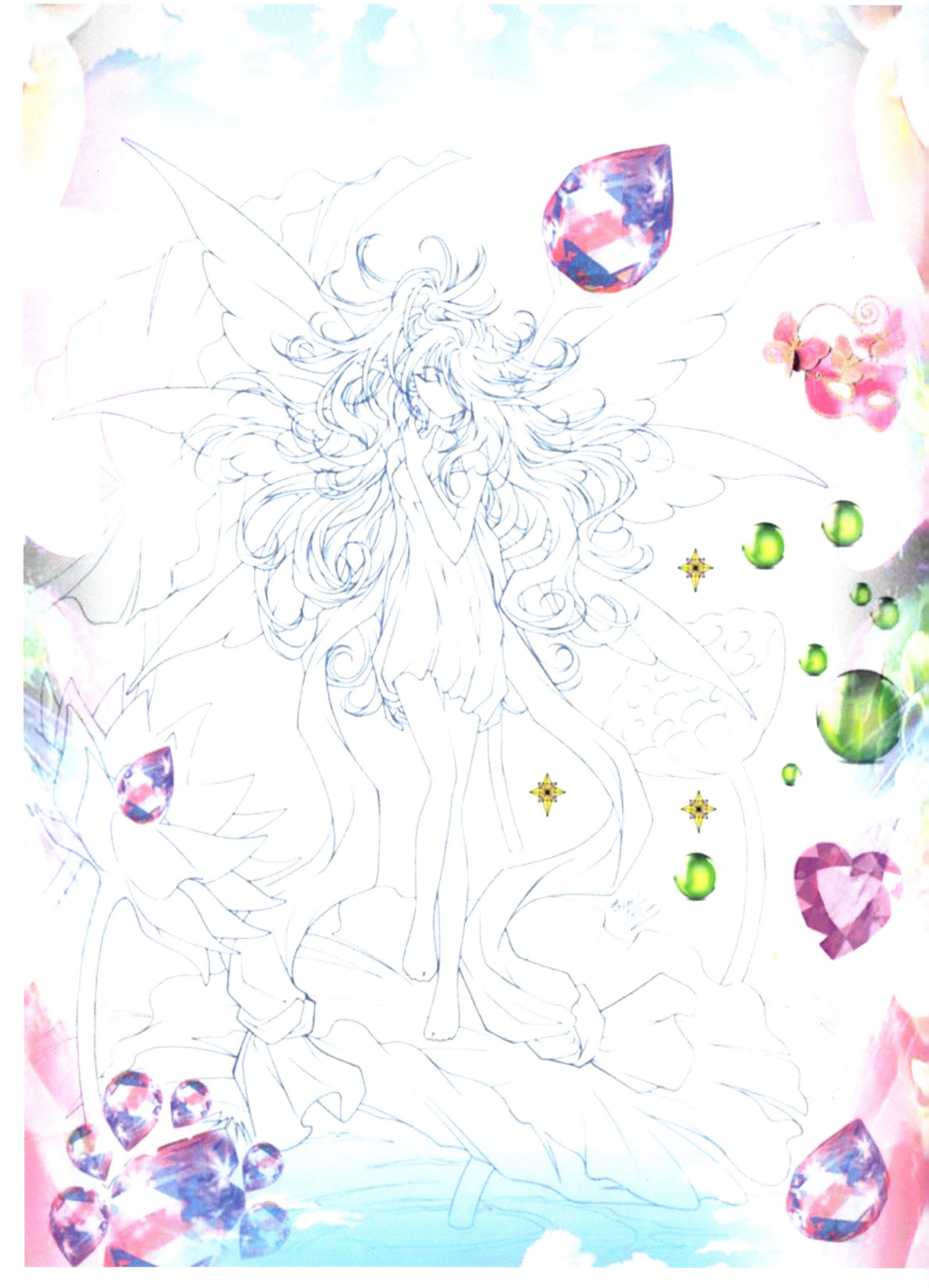

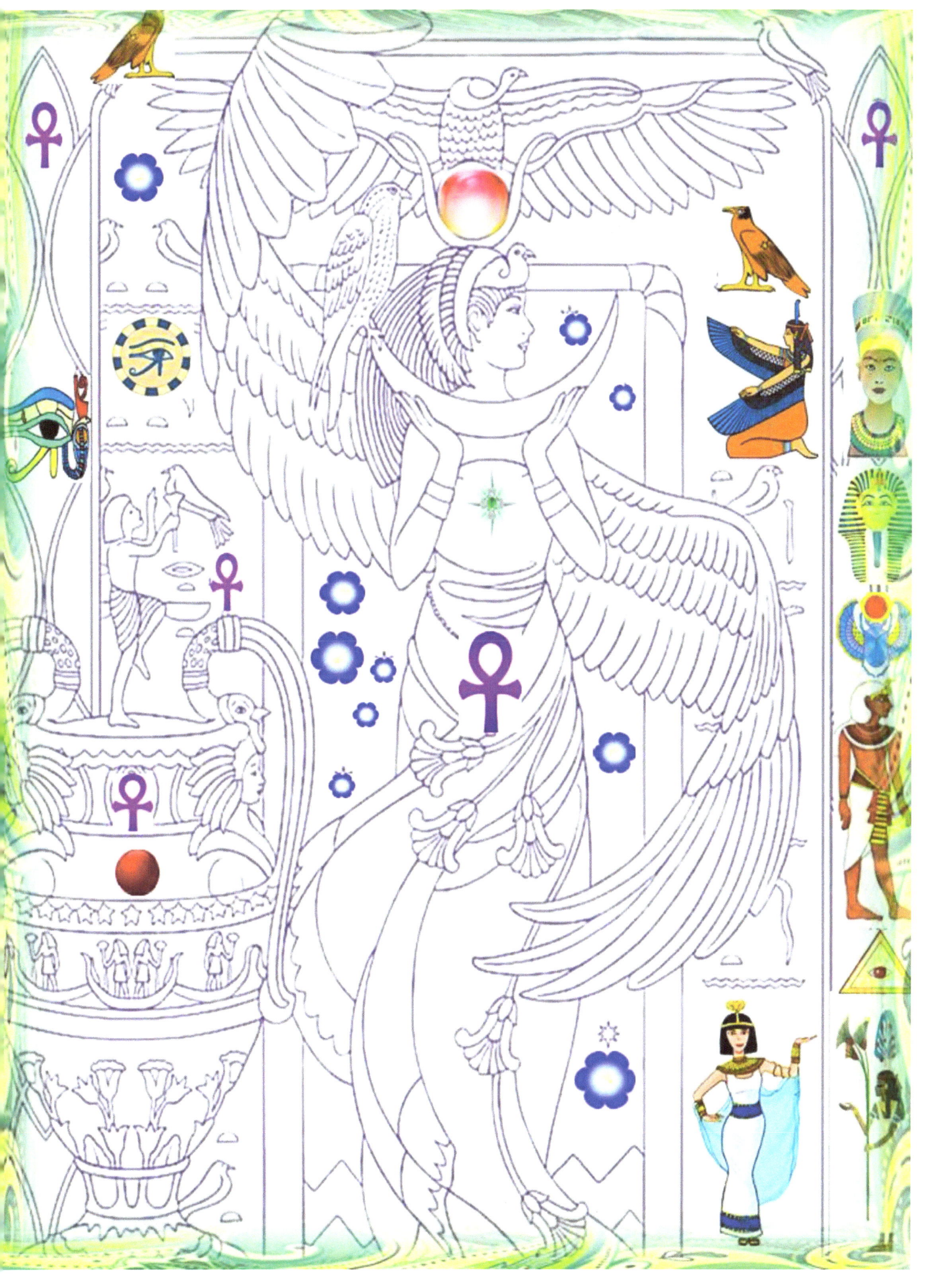

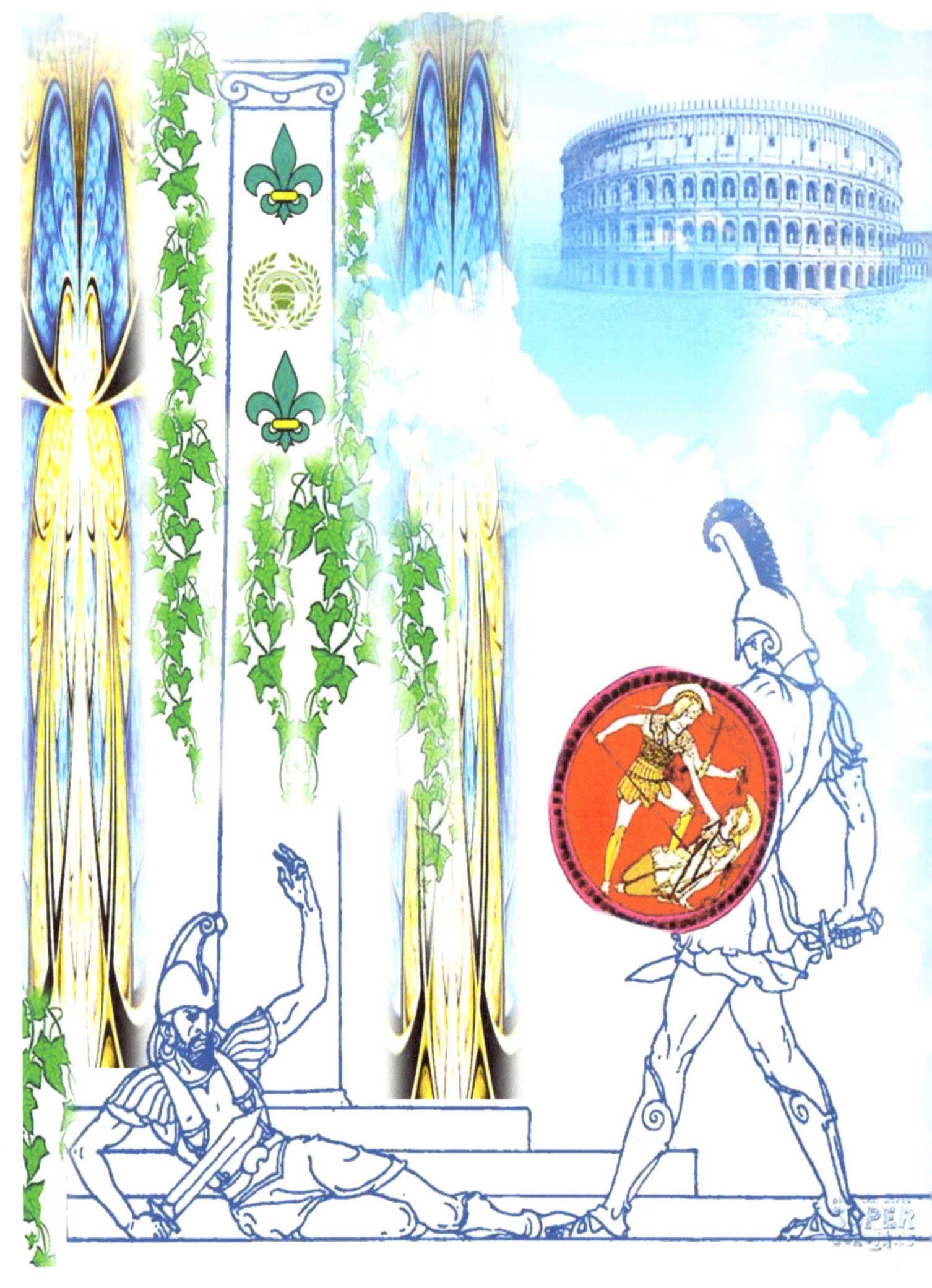

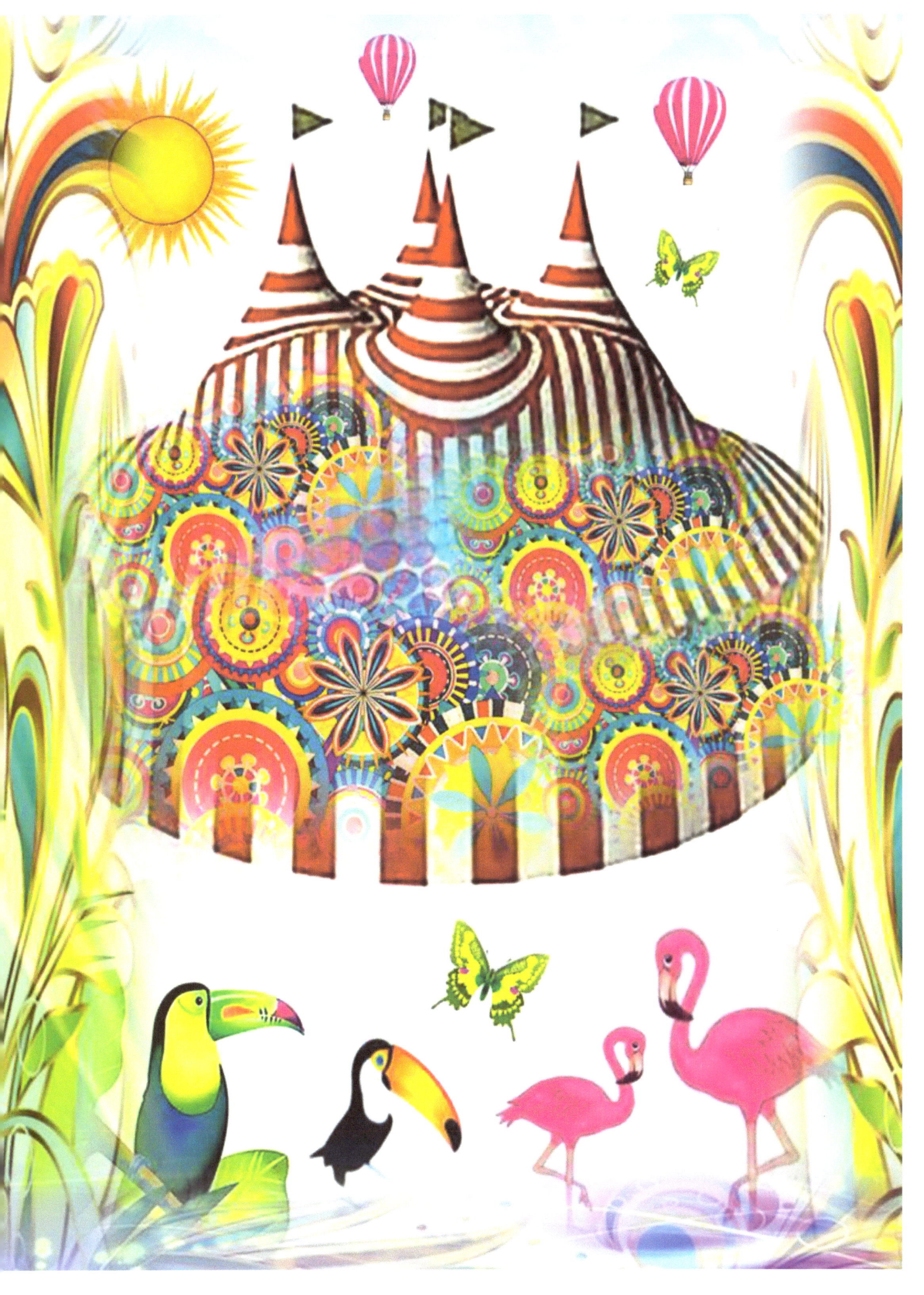

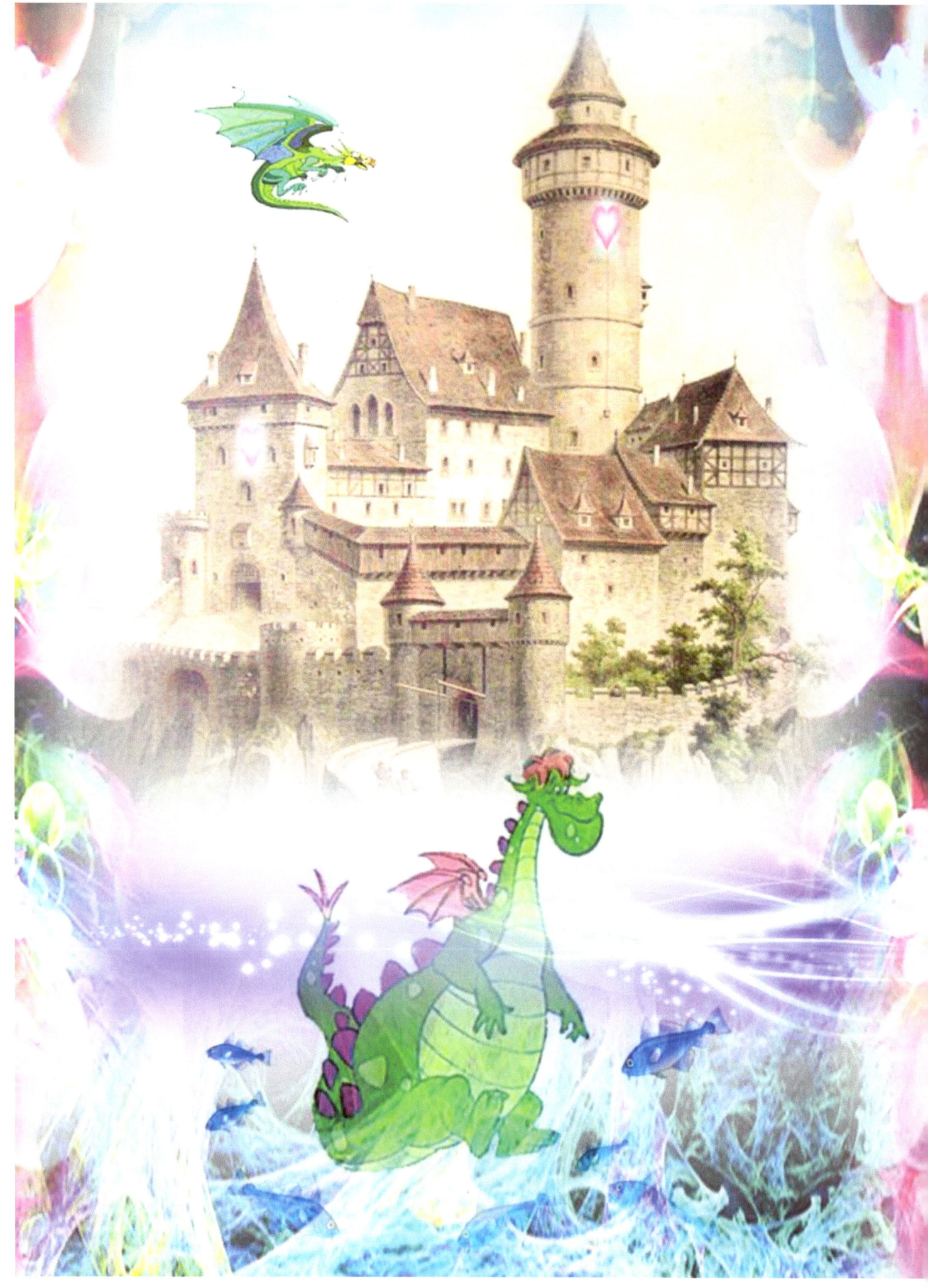

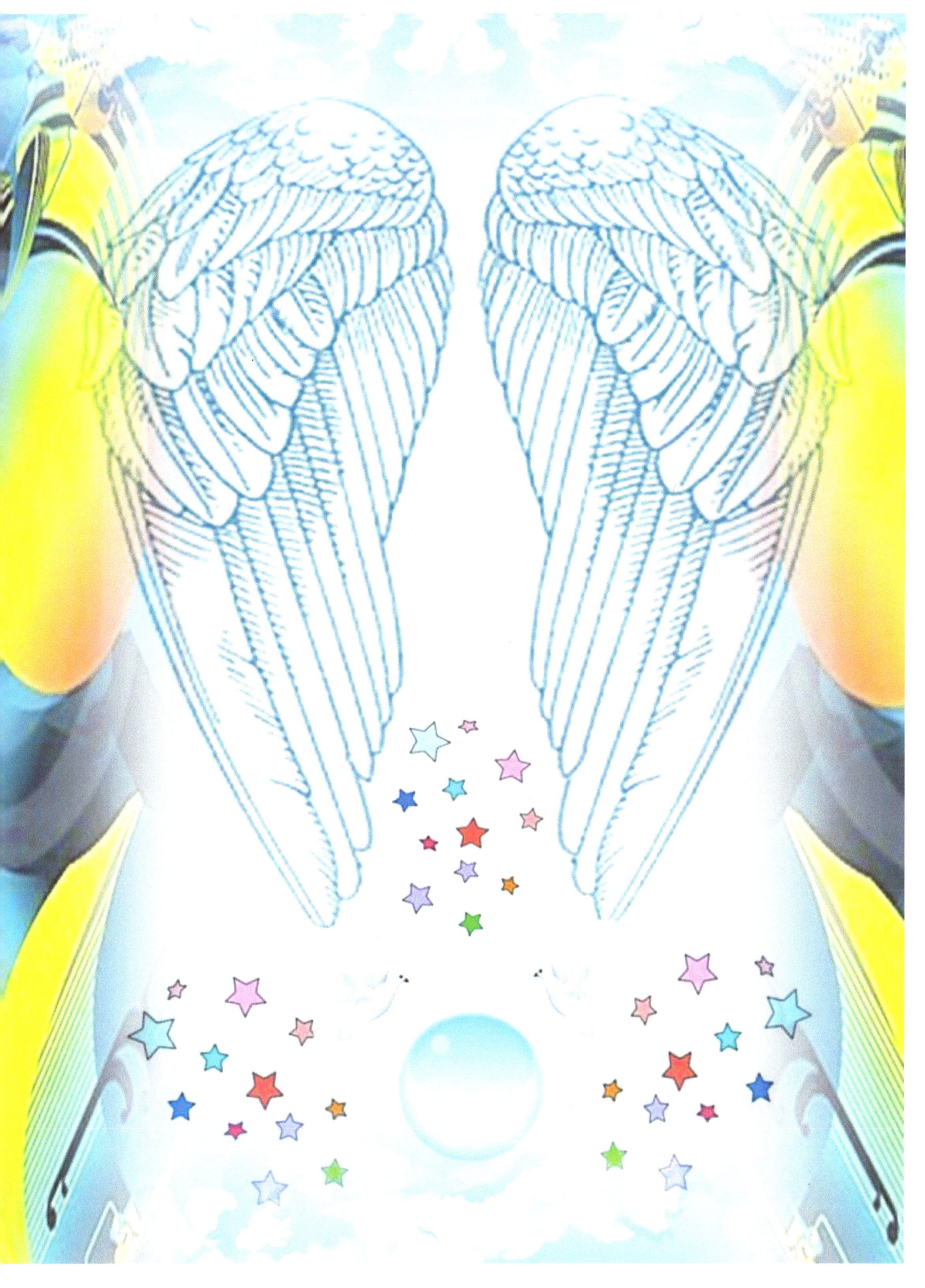

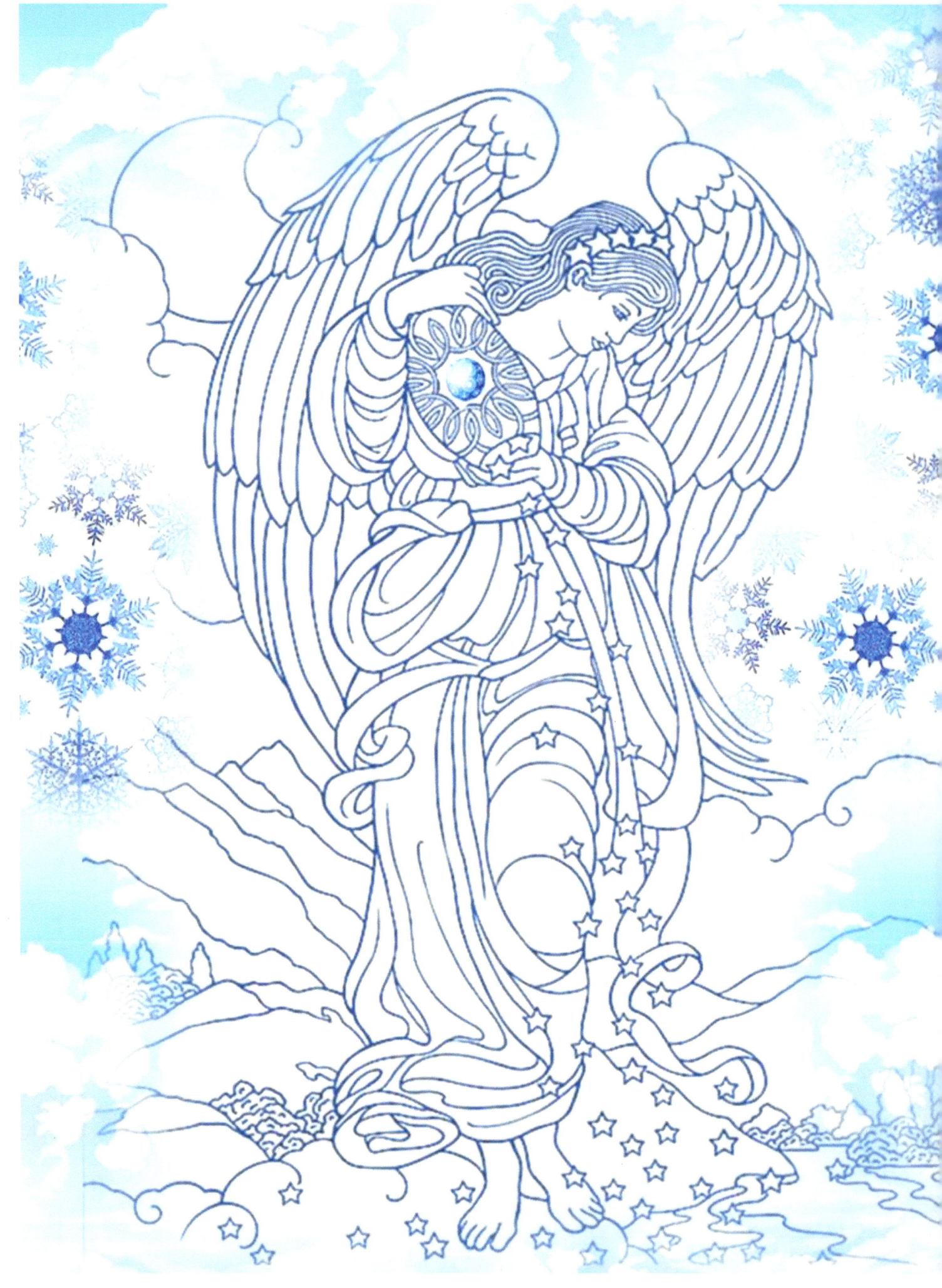

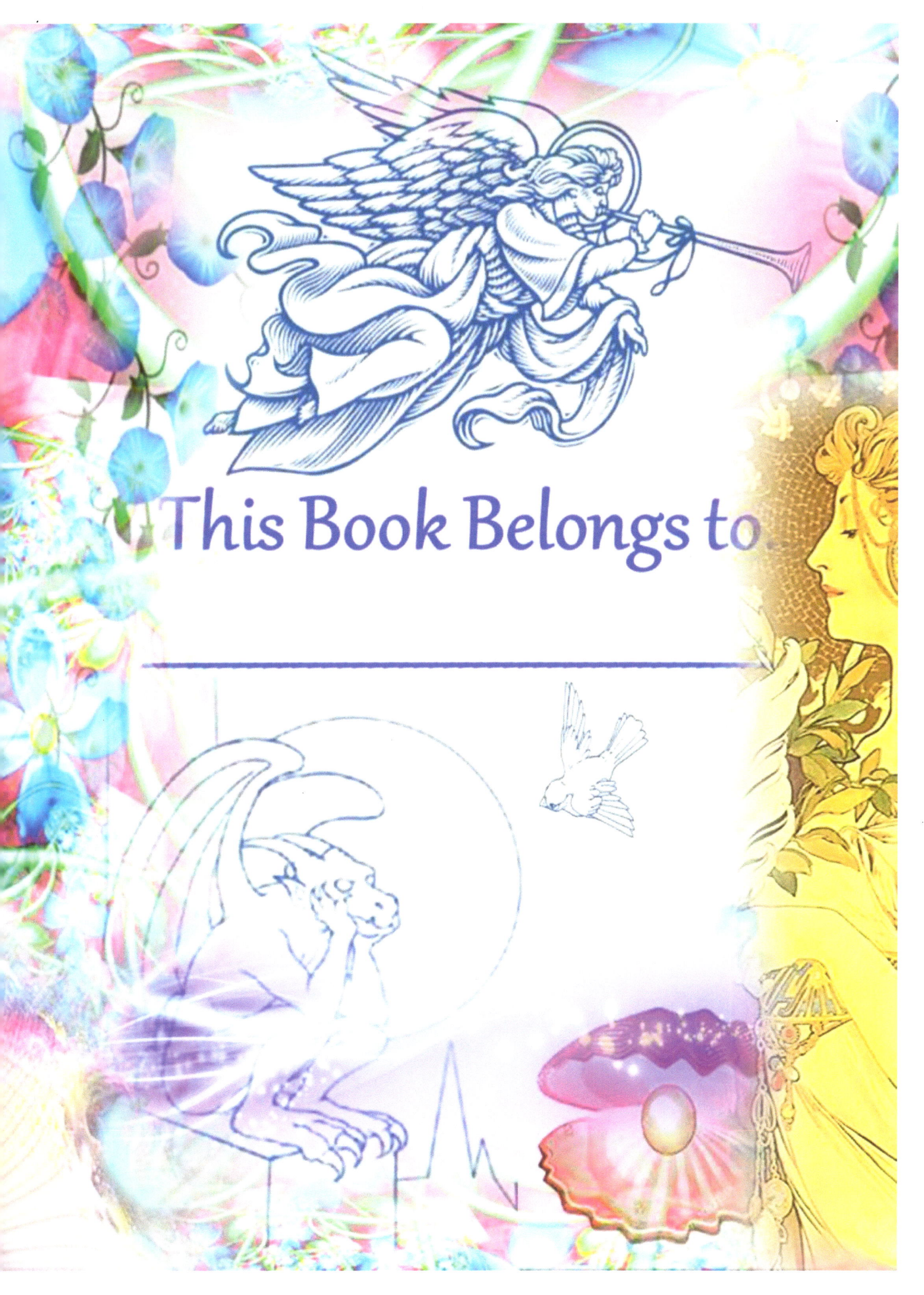

This Book Belongs to...